THE EAGLE CRIES

REVERSING THE LEGACY OF THE REBELLIOUS
1960s

Blanche B. Clayton

Dedication

To the memory and legacy of the late visionary

Archbishop Earl Paulk, Jr.

CONTENTS

Acknowledgements

I would like to thank the media (all forms), sociologists, mental health specialists, journalists, educators, church and political leaders. I have read your materials, documentaries, have seen videos, live broadcasts, attended your conferences, watched your interviews, and listened to what you had to say from many different perspectives about the events and experiences of social change in America from the 1960s through the 2000s. I also thank authors Archbishop Earl Paulk, Jr. and Dr. Robert Schuller for having the wisdom and courage to address biblical errors in scriptural interpretations, Anita Shreve and David Blankenhorn for addressing the challenges of fatherlessness and redefining motherhood, and other writers. Thank you to the songwriters, singers, producers, musicians, artists, entertainers and film makers of the 1960s era for capturing and documenting America's rebellious legacies. Your invaluable and infinite gifting provided a living legacy of the trials and crises of our evolution as a culture. Last but not least, to the comedians who helped to maintain a sense of humor throughout the many decades of America's unprecedented and ongoing dysfunction as a nation.

Foreword

To the parents and children of the millennium, this book is written to give you hope along with explanations for why you and your children are confronted with never before seen urgent social issues such as fatherlessness, human trafficking, no respect for authority figures, and child abandonment in American history. Additional examples are also written throughout the book to equip you with knowledge and information that will be needed for you to make conscious and wise choices today that will not only change your lives, but impact the lives of future generations. Your lives reflect generations who are lacking the knowledge of their true historical heritage. It is imperative that you know and understand how you became the product of generations of bad choices in the hope that you will break the current repetitive violent life cycle. Also, that you would end repeating the mistakes and failures of past generations.

Prior to the mid-sixties, decisions were based on and guided by strict adherence to moral principles which influenced the consciousness of the people. The consciousness of right and wrong was overshadowed and replaced by immoral practices which you have inherited. The continuous waves of immorality helped to change and reshape America to what it is today. This book will give you insight behind the thinking that led up to why the good intentions of the 1960s decisions have turned out badly for us in critical areas of our lives. Bad decisions fueled the disintegration of the family; planted the seeds that led to drug dependency; welcomed cohabitation as an acceptable alternative to marriage that initiated the sexual revolution.

It is my intention to offer you information at-a-glance with the hope that you will go deeper in finding more in-depth information to the causes of our present day turmoil and social turbulence.

THE EAGLE CRIES

The eagle cries to see how far America has drifted off shore

The eagle cries out turn around while there is still time

The eagle cries it is time to forgive from within and without

The eagle cries through tear-stained eyes, America awaken from your stupor

The eagle cries arise from the ashes of homelessness and fatherlessness

The eagle cries at the abandonment of its young left without a care

The eagle cries when its' young dies too soon

The eagle cries when indifference becomes the master ruler

The eagle cries when its young are doomed to a lifetime in time-out

The eagle's eyes are blurred by injustice in the streets

The eagle's eyes are blurred by frivolous priorities

The eagle's eyes are blinded by political biases and prejudices

The eagle's eyes are blinded by greed, materialism and lack of brotherhood

The eagle's eyes are blinded when human life is not a priority and is not valued

The eagle cries one nation, under God, indivisible, with liberty and justice for all, is still waiting

The "Eagle Cries" symbolizes the devastating conditions that are presently causing America to decay from the inside out. The eagle was chosen by the founding fathers as the nation's emblem because of the eagle's vision, great strength, long life, and might. America, once known around the world for its superb leadership, education and benevolence as a leading nation is now weakened. Bad decisions of the past has wounded, crippled and blinded the eagle's vision, power and strength. Yet, there remains hope to recover today by making right decisions.

INTRODUCTION

This book is written primarily to the millennial generation for their encouragement in taking the lead role in changing the current status quo of the present generation. It will give enlightenment and provide critical information to those of you who are the main inheritors of the present social chaos. Because America has meandered off course and has sailed into unchartered, unfamiliar and dangerous waters, it is imperative that it find and regain its intended course. Illustrations in this book will provide past and present models of family life and parenting practices for you to weigh in on the pros and cons of how family life has transitioned from the traditional model to the modern day family model. It will offer millennial families opportunities to make better informed choices by being knowledgeable of both past and present models that are necessary to make changes in the present inherited destructive legacies for their children and future generations.

This book will also give you insight on how America lost its course of direction. It will address key areas of their influence that has continued to plague the American culture. Their beginnings will be traced back to key decisions that were made during the youth rebellion of the 1960s that directly affect us today. We will explore specific areas that have been gravely impacted; and more importantly, we will examine the avenues that these critical decisions have traveled that carried over from decade to decade into the present time. Some decisions have expanded into the disintegration of the family, massive incarceration, human trafficking, child abandonment, and drug usage as an alternative form of religion. A major lesson in this for all of us is that we have the power of choice and we must use wisely. We are held captives by our bad choices of the past. They dictate and control our future if they are not corrected and replaced with good decisions. America did not suddenly find itself in a state of massive confusion in its major social institutions; this confusion is the result of long term bad decisions that generated and produced a negative cycle of consequences that continues to intensify and worsen.

The 1960s marked a significant change in the course and direction of our nation. It also signified the beginning of the rebirthing process for a new America. At that time there were many tidal waves of social change that took America by storm. Every wave carried its own unstoppable energies that stepped aside for no one. Every wave was unique and had its own focus, purpose and intent. They each had their own sound and battle cry. These waves of change are best described as a tsunami that carried the Civil Rights, Women's Rights, Gay Rights Movements and protests against the immorality of the Viet Nam War. These movements swept America's foundation clean from top to bottom.

Nothing was held sacred, untouchable or beyond their scope and reach to rebuild America's foundations predicated on love, creativity, equality, justice, and peace. Although separate, all shared the same destiny of achieving their human rights. As a collective body, they demanded their equal rights and fair treatment as American citizens.

America in the 1960s, historical events will be presented as resembling a woman who is suddenly travailing in child birth to simultaneously birth four mammoth social entities. Together they were able to successfully induce labor pains that were forceful enough to push themselves through the birth canal into a life of promised freedom and liberty. However, during the birthing process, critical pillars of America's foundation were cracked, badly torn, bruised and damaged. These social entities did not fully develop which resulted in massive societal discord and deformities, the likes of which we have never seen. Areas that received the most damage were family life, marriage (relationships), parenting children, and religion. These areas have grown and spiraled into enormous social dysfunctions and breakdowns.

More than four decades later, America is being challenged today with sorting through the rubble of its afterbirth. Our current challenges demand that we have open minds, creative minds, new perspectives, commitment and change how we think. We cannot meet our present challenges in the same mindset that created them. It is now our task to determine the extent of the damages that have occurred. We must voluntarily pay the price that is required of each of us in our collective efforts to help change the course of America. We must seize every opportunity to aid in America's recovery and making the world a better place to live.

Think

Rethink

Think Again!

Chapter One

Nothing Just Happens

The major social upheavals that America is now experiencing did not "just fall" on us. The social mishaps and changes that came about during the 1960s are responsible for our present day chaos and way of life. We must understand why our daily lives are constantly threatened by crime, violence and other hidden dangers that surround us. We must also recognize that every person is free to make his or her own choices and is responsible for the choices that they make. Our personal choices come with appropriate consequences whether our choices are good or bad, right or wrong, and is lived out accordingly. America is currently reaping over four decades of uninterrupted negative social consequences that have carried over to the present from the 1960s. Over time these consequences have developed into hostile thought patterns and inappropriate social behaviors that are now extremely volatile and dangerous. The millennial generation is confronted by long term consequences that produced generations that exhibits inhumane behaviors that go far beyond normal expectations, and threaten the quality and safety of our existence today. These challenges include the abandonment of children, sound parenting practices, heightened crime and violence rates, divorce, fatherlessness, proliferation of drug usage and sales, loss of respect for authority figures, loss of positive male role models, and the perpetual demand to build more prisons.

What will be the impact on the lives of children not yet born (who must not be born) into a society that is already filled with hostile and chaotic conditions should the present social living conditions remain unchanged? Without America making a change, the future of unborn children is dismal. The unborn will be destined to expand the present existing consciousness which can only take us into deeper levels of chaos that could expand far beyond what is already here. As more and more children are born today, they will fall prey and become victims of chaotic living conditions that were created by the previous generations. Our present moment in history serves as a compass telling us where we are today and is pointing to where we hope we can be in the future. We must aggressively turn our attention in the direction where immediate changes are needed. The task of turning our present challenges away from further adversity is our choice to make.

America's Regeneration

In the 1960s, America as a young nation succumbed to the high pressured demands for change that were made by the rebellious youth culture. America's firm image and unbending nature was transformed to reflect the temperament and distinctive qualities of the youth. The spirit of America modeled and was similar to the toddler stage of human development known as ages and stages. In the toddler stage young children exercise their independence and free will to do things on their own without the assistance of adults. This stage is symbolic of the 1960s as the youth in America rebelled against all recognized and established authority figures. To help them gain and establish their independence, the approach they used was spontaneous, combative, and confrontational. Their first line of rebellion was against family leadership-- their parents and elders that expanded throughout all of society. Any of the existing and organized establishments, they wanted no part of it; family, learning institutions, businesses, churches, etc. all represented structure.

Exploration and Discovery

As America was changing, it modeled a second stage of toddler development know as exploration. Young children are inquisitive about their environment; their tolerance for having restrictions are low; their inquisitive nature is to tackle and explore their environment nonstop; their focus is to find welcomed and unwelcomed buried treasures. Toddlers can be easily provoked as they stumble upon hidden treasures. For the toddler, any resistance encountered is fuel for their untiring energies. Resembling inquisitive toddlers, the youth culture through their explorations of America's social structure made some discoveries concerning the lack of care for the environment; and its overall unsatisfactory living conditions and practices. The more the youth explored and the deeper they looked to find the answers to their concerns about the disparities in their findings;   dissatisfaction grew, and the more untrusting of the answers that were given by authority figures. Their lack of trust in authority posed a major threat that formed a gap and breakdown in their relationships.

The youth met adult resistance with resistance, and the confrontation between the "old mindsets" against the "new mindsets" were set into motion. Conservative adults and the youth were in opposition to the other. The gap between generations grew wider and wider which resulted in the formation and development of the "youth culture" that still divides generations today. Perhaps the outcome of our history could have been different if both sides had learned the value of showing respect for each other's different point of view.

The youth culture became a force to be reckoned with. America was under attack by the youth's demands for structural change. The youth intentionally launched attacks against what was labeled as "the establishment". The youth were determined not to be restrained by any organized group or institution. Every social institution in America came under attack if any flaws were detected. While in the midst of confrontations, things of extrinsic worth and value can get lost, damaged or destroyed when excessive and continuous probes are made by undeveloped and untrained eyes. I believe this is what happened to America as a result of the youth uprising. Valuable social values were demoralized and destroyed because the youth had not matured enough to understand their purpose and the depth of their meaning. Their concentration focused on changing the exterior not understanding the interior damage their decisions would later have on the future. The conflict between generations influenced how America began to grow. The youth had made their mark which also marked the beginning stages of the reshaping of the American culture and values as we know it today. Rebellious and strong-willed youth were now "leading" the way in America's revolution from conservatism.

Taking the lead, the 1960s era initiated and brought about fundamental changes in the American story. Led by middle and upper middle class children who rebelled against their parents, elders, and the society of their day, a rebellion called the "hippie movement" had emerged. The youth had high aspirations and hopes of changing the way human beings lived. Their quest began by exuding actions and behaviors that were out of kilter from the status quo of their parents and society. They challenged societal norms and the authority of their parents and elders. They also rejected their parents and elders leadership, lifestyles, morals, and social values. This level of opposition, denial and rejection by the youth must have caused their parents much heartache, pain, suffering and grief.

Their rebellious nature led me to ask the question, "What did the youth find that was so disenchanting about their parents' lifestyles and society that caused them to be relentless in their quest to strip and walk away from the opportunities they had been afforded?" "Were they living in poor neighborhoods?" "Was the economy bad?" "No." They lived in good neighborhoods, the economy was very good, their parents were first generation college graduates and homeowners. It seemed a reasonable expectation of their parents that they would go to college, get a job in corporate America, buy a home, marry, and raise a family as well. It was the general consensus of the people at that time, that children from upper and middle class families were already living the American Dream that others desired to have.

However, from the youth's perspectives, their parents' lifestyles were not modeling open expression and creativity that reflected the true meaning and purpose for living. They perceived their parents lifestyles as limited, based on uniformity, and conformity to the same familiar everyday rituals and routines. They wanted no part of this perceived cookie cutter lifestyle. The youth believed there was more to life than what was lived out in front of them by their parents, they desired more. They desired the freedom to creatively express themselves openly, to create a different lifestyle for themselves, and a different way to parent their children.

Marriage Under Scrutiny

As a result of the youth's growing dissatisfaction of their everyday life, three of America's main pillars—marriage, family and religious institutions were realigned and greatly altered that are almost unrecognizable today. The youth sought new alternatives in what they believed to be better ways that would improve the institution of marriage. In their findings from observing their parents' marriages and society, marriage from their perspective was too confining. Meanwhile, alternative lifestyles with couples living together outside of marriage were progressively growing. Cohabitation rates were very low in the sixties but became a huge trendsetter that is an acceptable lifestyle for modern day couples.

The institution of marriage suffered another blow with the emergence of the sexual revolution. The promotion of free love and open sex was glamorized and served as an attractive piece of the fringe benefits package of the popular unwed lifestyle. Couples wanted the freedom to enjoy sex without the fear of procreation. Married couples also wanted the freedom to enjoy sex outside of their marriage. Fueled by these trends, the idea of free sex and love was quickly packaged, marketed and sold to the entire American public. To young parents of the millennial, the 1960s parents did not suddenly stop parenting their children. The institution of marriage and the family was targeted by the youth culture whose desire was to parent their children differently.

Changing Parental Priorities

We are at our wits end today wondering what factors created the conflict between parents and children that split them apart. We are also perplexed over the longevity of the unresolved conflict and disputes in the parent-child relationship that is now a major social problem of the family, schools and society. From their own personal experiences and observations of how children in the sixties had been parented, the new leaders found a need to change the limitations and restrictions that restrictive parenting placed on children. Consequently, the youth rejected their parents' way of parenting in order to try something new and creative. They preferred a more liberal way to parent their children because of the restrictions that had been placed on them when they were children.

Surprisingly, something phenomenal happened along the way to hinder reaching their goal--the declining interest of parents in parenting their children. Parents interest in parenting grew less and less as the preoccupation with their personal interests grew more and more. As parental interests continued to increase, raising children soon was no longer parents' number one priority. Rather, the self-interests of parents became their number one priority and their children moved into second place. This was a radical change in the traditional family.

Spiritual Insufficiency

America's religious leaders were sorely criticized by the younger generation for not giving enlightenment that was sufficient in meeting their spiritual needs necessary for them to make social changes. Religion and spiritual growth in America felt by many in the sixties had become stagnant and irrelevant to their day. Dr. Robert Schuller, Christian theologian agreed with this assumption in his book "Self-Esteem-The New Reformation, … the church may be in serious error in substance, style or spirit" (Schuller, 1982, p.74). He further noted that the institutional church would continue off course if correction was not made. Conformity to the status quo was the main by-product of religious teachings, practices, rules and customs. Organized religion was the only offering that was given by the church to traditional families.

The youth was hungering for personal transformation and the unfolding of deeper spiritual insight and enlightenment. They wanted insight that would help them to move forward in their quest to change their present way of life in America. They opened themselves to explore different religions, along with other ways and means to find inspiration and spiritual enlightenment.

Their unmet spiritual need thrust America into the midst of a spiritual revolution where there were no limits placed on the human mind and spirit. To help show Americans the way to true spiritual enlightenment, religious leaders from around the world filled the street corners, airports and other public places with proselytizers offering solace and support to meet the youth's spiritual appetites. This spiritual smorgasbord included Moonies, Hare Krishna, gurus, Sri Chinmay, Buddhists, etc. Also, rather than look to traditional religion, the youth looked to music and the arts for inspiration. Rolling Stone Magazine captured this phenomenon noting that pop icons were now the new leaders of this spiritual pack through their art, poetry, entertainment and music (Khan, George-Warren, and Dhal, 1998).

Alternative to Religion

Also, with the experimental and recreational use of drugs as an alternative to the traditional religious beliefs and practices of their parents, the youth had finally fulfilled their spiritual appetite. Drug usage quickly permeated college campuses through private off-site parties. As the word spread, using drugs to get high became the fastest growing alternative to religion among the young. Drug usage swept throughout mainstream America like a raging fire destroying anyone and anything that crossed its path. With the newly found drug frenzy to find inner enlightenment came consequences that released exaggerated and narcissistic behaviors, vanity, and greed into the culture. Also, with the experimental and recreational usage of drugs came the inability to manage and control the side effects it was having on the youth culture. Through drug dependency, drug sales became the fastest growing illegal way to make a quick buck. It undermined the American Dream of gaining wealth through getting an education and hard work. Wealth was never to be achieved by creating a drug addicted society. Getting ahead was not to be gained by weakening and destroying the lives of its citizens for profit.

Social Crisis

Changes in America's primary social institutions became major contributors for the social decline in America. Their missions were redefined, expanded, and reversed. For example, our schools were expanded to not only educate children but to become more inclusive of the family's needs by incorporating into their daily operations many of the duties held by parents. America soon lost the capacity to control its social conditions such as drug dependency and failing education that were growing at accelerated speeds and were producing consequences where America had no answers. This rapid social outgrowth rate has produced the greatest unforeseen social challenges of our time. Our present social ills far exceeds the previous generations, and have reached an overflow in our society that is harmful and toxic.

The harvest that America is reaping today is from the radical seeds of rebellion that was sown and planted in the 1960s changed the hearts and minds of the American people. After the initial planting of the radical seeds they multiplied and have reproduced over four decades of toxic consequences which are now interwoven into the inner fabric of the American way of life that is widely accepted today as the "new normal".

America's New Normal

Sex before marriage was not a normal practice in the American way of life . Couples were married before they had children. Parents were the primary caregivers of their children. Policemen were friends and protectors of the community. Parents and teachers were positive role models for children. Fathers were living in the home and provided for the needs of their children. Lifestyles today cope with sexual predators; athletes, television and movie stars are the role models for children; loving and caring parents are seen as weak and their lives boring and unnecessary; the fear of being ordinary plagues the young; drugs and human trafficking; hostile police officers, teachers and parents; continual high crime and frequents acts of violence; fear of committed relationships; single mothers coping with the cries of their young children for their daddies are all part of the new American landscape. Is the "new normal" a way of

life that we want to continue giving sustainability?
Does the "new normal" provide us with sustainable and
stress-free security while going about our daily
routines? Are we satisfied with the new functionality of
our current social institutions?

Sex Casualties

The choice to promote free love and open sex planted
seeds that released the human sexual potential that was
kept under restraint and was hidden. Sex seeds like
drug seeds have multiplied, expanded, and grown into
unthinkable social consequences such as violent sex
crimes, molestation, infidelity, promiscuity, disease,
pornography, human sex trafficking, and fatherlessness.
For the protection of children, background checks have
been instituted to identify sexual predators. Sexual
predators live among us as our next door neighbors.
Once sexual freedom was released, it removed the
requirement for couples to marry in order to have sex.
Freedom carries with it the added responsibility to do
the right thing and to respect the rights of others.

A Call to Take Action

The initial intention and vision of the sixties was to
open a passageway of love, peace, and sharing for
everybody to have all things in common. Bad decisions
of the past has led America to its present destination.
What we do know for sure is that the lessons we have
learned from our present experiences give us enough

insight to know that we must go back and reexamine the foundational pillars that our lives were previously built upon, to make better informed decisions and to adjust and correct our bad decisions. Also, taking a step back will help us to find and regain our sense of purpose, and set the right priorities for the future. Taking a pause will also break the repetitious cycle of wrong thinking that has produced decades of unfavorable results. The younger and the older generations working side-by-side and hand-in-hand so that together we can make the right changes that will be for the good of all.

Truth and honesty with love must become the new normal in putting America back on the right course. To help us in transforming our nation we must first transform ourselves by collectively practicing the concept to think, rethink and think again every time we are faced with a decision, large or small. It will help to remind us of our commitment to change old thought patterns, and to create a fresh awareness of the new direction that we are undertaking. With consistent practice in our daily decisions we will gradually break the cycle of unconsciously reinforcing negative thought patterns and become more and more conscious of right and healthy ways to think and make good decisions.

Imagine with me: How many of our social problems would disappear if children were properly parented? What impact would parenting have on the incarceration rate? Would America's high school graduation rates sky-rocket? What would be the impact of parental engagement on our social atrocities? Would the quality of family life be enhanced if fathers were back in the home? What impact could we expect if all working fathers received higher wages that would meet their families' financial needs? How would America benefit from a religious system that transformed into acceptable spiritual practices that offered love and hope; provided relevant insight for meeting everyday decisions; worked closer with other helping professions in restoring and reconciling families; removed gender roles, encouraged creativity, removed religious labels and was inclusive of all its citizenry?

Nothing just happens, the seeds that we plant today will grow and produce tomorrow's harvest.

CHAPTER TWO

SOUNDS OF THE MILLENNIAL GENERATION

Currently we are experiencing some disturbing unrest in every critical area of our lives in America. Many of these disturbances have come as a result of major damage that occurred during the birthing process of social change when America was a young and growing nation. Having a strong determination to change the status quo in the 1960s, America entered into childbirth unprepared and enthralled in major conflict. However, the sixties generation forged ahead in labor without aid and assistance by rejecting pre-existing knowledge and information available to them. They chose to give birth to change on their own by seeking alternative ways. We will examine some of these major alternatives and methods that were used to make changes in key areas of the American fabric that has caused some serious internal leakage that is now gushing. We cannot delay addressing these internal tears that took place in the birthing canal because they are causing us to rapidly disintegrate today at a rapid rate from within.

Fast forwarding, in a 2010 report the Children's Defense Fund printed an article, "Moments in America for all Children," that gives us a close look at an area in America's fabric that is in urgent need of repair. Findings in this report identified key areas of concerns that are found with our children.

"Every second a public school student is suspended.

Every 11 seconds a high school student drops out.

Every 19 seconds a child is arrested.

Every 19 seconds a baby is born to an unmarried mother.

Every 20 seconds a public school student is corporally punished.

Every 32 seconds a baby is born into poverty.

Every 41 seconds a child is confirmed as abused or neglected.

Every 42 seconds a baby is born without health insurance.

Every minute a baby is born to a teen mother.

Every minute a baby is born at low birth rate.

Every 4 minutes a child is arrested for a drug offense.

Every 7 minutes a child is arrested for a violent crime.

Every 18 minutes a baby dies before his or her first birthday.

Every 45 minutes a child or teen is killed by a firearm.

Every 3 hours a child or teen commits suicide.

Every 6 hours a child is killed by abuse or neglect.

Every 15 hours a mother dies from complications of childbirth or pregnancy. "

The sound of the Millennial Generation are children who are characterized as having or showing no feeling of being remorseful after committing wrongful acts to the life and property of others. Gangs rule our streets and the gang mentality has become the lifestyle in America. Children of the millennium have asked some hard questions that have gone unanswered such as, Why should I go to college when I can sell drugs and make more money? Why do I need an education when I can join a gang? Further questions have also been asked such as, Why marry? Why settle for one relationship when I can have as many as I want? Life decisions and lifestyles today are based on "getting" without having to make any commitments. An alternative lifestyle in this sense means living life without having to pay a price. Young educated working women are frustrated in finding a mate who is willing to commit to being in a relationship. Fatherlessness and single parent families have become normal alternative lifestyles as well. Marriage has now become uncommon in America's new landscape.

The sound of human sex trafficking can be clearly heard without regard to age or gender. Young children and women are turning up missing daily in our country. Pornography and prostitution are out of control and very challenging for law enforcement to manage. It has been said that whatever outside of man that can satisfy his human appetites will eventually control him.

The millennial sound continues with the inclusion of children in America's fastest growing prison population.

According to recent reports, America now has the largest prison population in the world. Today when young children are asked the question, what do they want to be when they grow up? Many will answer, "I want to go to jail" since jail is where their family members live, they want to go and be with them.

Drug use, abuse and sales are another major cry of the Millennial Generation. The sale and consumption of drugs, legal and illegal have lulled Americans to sleep, meanwhile our precious liberties are slipping away. Has the use of drugs deadened our pain due to natural childbirth to the degree that we became less sensitive and unaware that the important things in our lives were slipping away? Did the influence of drugs confuse our priorities? Did drugs undermine and destroy our level of trust in family life, personal relationships and government? Did it help to destroy foundations on which our lives were built? Did drugs influence and confuse our purpose for living? Did drugs distract us by putting our attention on passing things such as consumerism, rather than on developing our personal inner strength and character? Did the promotion of drug usage in the sixties create a significant shift from the youth's initial intention of developing a more liberal nation where bringing about love, peace, human worth and social goodness was the goal? Instead drugs contrarily created a counterculture of addiction, lying, stealing and killing that has become America's normal way of life. People are now expected to lie rather than tell the truth. A person is considered abnormal for telling the truth and taking responsibility for his own actions.

Another sound that is causing unrest to the Millennial Generation is the decades of children who have never been parented by their biological parents. Did child care entities successfully do the job of parents? What were the changes in family life that caused teenage pregnancies to skyrocket? Additionally, crime and violence committed by youth soared. What were the changes that contributed to the widespread disrespect for all authority figures (parents, teachers & police)? What caused children to suddenly kill their parents, shoot up the schools, friends and their teachers? What has angered America's children to the point where they would rather die than to live?

The millennials are without the luxury of repeating the mistakes of previous generations that has gone before them. Your challenge is not to follow the status quo of today, but to do what is right. The millennial sounds are symbolic of ongoing generational consequences that have been passed on by the rebellion of the 1960s. These sounds are echoing to the millennial generation that it is time to make a change now.

Chapter Three

CHILDREN: AMERICA'S BIGGEST LOSERS

The vision of the 1960s for families called for a better and a more liberating way to parent children that would develop and enhance future parenting practices and values. The youth's primary goal as future parents was not to duplicate the traditional and restrictive child rearing practices of their parents. As a result of their eliminating all childrearing values and practices of the past caused the greatest harm and damage to occur in the lives of children and their families. A significant shift also occurred after women gained their equal rights. The role of women transitioned from stay-at-home moms to the new status of working mothers. For mothers to achieve higher education goals, careers and social aspirations, children lost the status as their number one priority. Additionally, first time working mothers' primary responsibilities and focus conflicted with their role as parents. This conflict of interest created a huge vacuum (lack of availability) in the lives of children and the family, and was a key factor in changing the way children would be parented.

Child Abandonment

As parents roles within the family were continually shifting, the children became more and more openly defiant, and willfully chose to disobey their parents. As a consequence, parents continued to lose their ability to influence and control their children. Soon children with working parents were socially labeled abandoned or children with absentee parents. In the entire history of America the absence and abandonment of children by their parents was never a practice of the family. Also with the absence of parents and the loss of priority for children, the lack of parenting children began taking its root in the American culture. As a result of the lack of investment in the lives of children, all of society is now paying the price for their deficiencies. With the lack of parenting, time, and attention to their ongoing nurturing, children began to lack life's basic skills and were yet, prematurely left on their own by their parents to face critical life issues and situations. Children's destructive behavior can camouflage a much deeper and underlying problem that lies beneath the surface in their lack of development of those innate qualities and traits necessary for them to thrive as healthy human beings. In light of the transitioning of the role and structure of the family, we must pause and ask ourselves who is raising America's children? Whose responsibility is it now to parent the children? The missing role of parents has produced great stress unseen in the mental and emotional development of children today.

Restrictive Parenting

To provide uninformed parents with deeper insight into parenting practices of the past; and to help you to gain a better understanding of the subject, listed below are a few examples of the 1960s "restrictive" parenting practices along with a brief explanation of the values that were instilled in children.

1. Children were their parents' number one priority. Children were under adult supervision at all times and were the recipients of their parents' undivided attention.

2. Children were taught to ask their parents for permission "before" any action was taken on their part in both large and small matters (i.e. whenever they left the house, and at what age could they start dating?)
   Through the "ask first" practice, the parents' goal was to teach their children how to acknowledge and show respect for authority figures, and to teach them the purpose and meaning of authority.

3. Children were not permitted exclusive rights in choosing their friends. The final selection of friends came under the scrutiny and the watchful eye of the parents. Watchful parents did not permit their children to befriend other children who were known to exhibit disrespectful and inappropriate behaviors.

4. Effective parenting was also predicated on the practice that children should be "seen and not heard." Children were not allowed to participate or be in the same room when adult conversations

were in progress. This practice prevented children from premature exposure to adult materials, language and behaviors. Today, experts in early childhood education recognize this concept, young children learn by observing and modeling what they see and hear adults do and say. In the past, this practice was also considered as a deferred privilege for children until they reached maturity and the age for their own consent.

5. "Do as I say and not as I do." This was a dual practice that was hard for both parents and children to effectively implement. In this practice, parental attempts were to discourage children from modeling after inappropriate adult behavior and language that they may have accidently seen or heard. Parents focused on building better and stronger character traits within their children. Their stringent ongoing efforts of intervention were to help prevent their children from inheriting and modeling after their flawed character traits, habits and weaknesses as parents. Parents wanted their children to be better people and not fall into the same trap or vice that had ensnared them. However, as children grew older, the practice of "do as I say and not as I do" created the greatest misunderstanding between parents and children. Children viewed this practice as a double standard and hypocrisy. As the old saying

goes, they preferred parents who practiced what they preached.

Nonetheless, the youth of the 1960s rejected these parenting practices and values for the opportunity to create their own practices. The youth wanted parenting practices that (1) provided their children new and better options that were not given to them by their parents; (2) practices that eliminated restrictions imposed by adults; and (3) practices that focused on the free will and autonomy of children that empowered them with the freedom to choose. Experimenting with this open, unscripted model as a base for parenting, has led to children systematically and methodically losing parents as their primary caregivers. Under the new developing liberal and modern style of parenting, the status of children has been in constant motion. As parents became more and more aggressive in their personal pursuits and activities, children also became less and less the center of their parents' time and attention. This practice resulted in a massive growth in the child care industry.

Moment of Decision

Childcare historically was for military wives whose husbands had gone off to war, and for those wives whose husbands had lost their lives in combat. The increased use of daycare is another major contributor to children being America's biggest losers. In the late 1960s, former stay-at-home moms mentally and emotionally anguished over separating from their children and being forced to trust the care of their children to others. Mothers questioned whether they were doing the right thing. In 1972 the practice of placing children into organized childcare rapidly accelerated in a growth rate that far exceeded other industries as mothers in record numbers joined the work force. Employment in child care that same year created 375,000 jobs (Goodman, 1995, p.3). The fact that children in America were primarily parented by their biological parents now has over four decades of children who have never been parented by their biological parents is an amazing outcome. The high ranking task of caring for children who were once the primary responsibility of their parents has now been outsourced to childcare providers.

Declining Role of Parents

The outsourcing of childcare for children has become a widespread practice for parents that is driven and motivated not only by work related but non-work related needs of parents (i.e. dating and having free time). Parents were younger and more immature and the role of the parent took on audacious and unreceptive character not known heretofore. It was unthinkable and unacceptable for parents to drop off their children unauthorized at local churches on Sundays while they went shopping at the mall; and without being a member of the congregation. I recall an incident in an apartment

35

complex where I lived, that this small child went door to door knocking on the neighbors' doors asking if she could spend the night. When she got to my door I asked, "Where is your mother? Why isn't your mother doing the asking for you?" The child replied that her mother had informed her that she was going out on a date, later needed some privacy, and that she needed to find a place to spend the night on her own. The growth of this bold and unwholesome practice of parents is threaded throughout the fabric of the American culture (i.e., sporting programs, after school programs, and other community programs that serve children).

Systematically, parents have detached themselves more and more from their role as primary caregivers. Parents today frown at the notion of being referenced as the primary one who is held responsible for what happens to their children. This change in parental attitudes and responsibilities are reflective of decades of "children having children" when they were young who themselves were never parented. Teenage pregnancies in the 1980s rose to over 200 percent (Births to Teenagers in the United States, 2001, p.5). "Babies having babies" became the catch word of the day. The neglect and abuse of children also rose to over 300 percent in the 1980s as well and was declared a national epidemic against children by the federal government (Center for Disease Control). The late 1970s and 1980s were turbulent years for children and families in America.

Parental Impact on Schools

America has maintained a steady course in transitioning the traditional role of biological parents as the natural and primary caretakers of their children, into institutionalized care by childcare providers. What should be realized and understood on a broader scale is to dispel the mythical illusion that childcare providers and school teachers serve as substitute parents for raising our children. Schools and other learning institutions were not designed or created to raise America's children. Their mission and purpose is to facilitate the learning process and to provide children with an education. This lack of understanding has opened a huge gap between home and school that has caused the schools to greatly deviate from their mission. Also, this gap has hindered and aided in the breakdown of the schools' capacity to perform more proficiently. As a former childcare director of preschoolers, I often reminded uninformed and bewildered young parents to recognize and understand the concept that education "does not don't raise children; they educate them."

With the constant growth of outsourcing childcare, the new generation of America's children have only known the care that has been provided to them exclusively by unknown childcare workers. In this childcare arrangement lies inconsistent childcare caused by high staff turnovers, absenteeism, and low paying salaries. Early childhood experts agree that children thrive best through building and maintaining trusting, stable, loving and consistent relationships with adults. Organized childcare for children is big business and has very quickly become the common household practice for the care of children by America's younger families.

Self-Care

New roles and responsibilities within the family shifted children to become their own self-care providers which also shifted the role of the parents as their primary caregivers. Children's new responsibilities and duties included managing their own care and needs (cooking, laundry); becoming more independent and less dependent on their parents (homework, free time); taking the lead role as decision makers with limited or no parental input and guidance (spending, social activities). Few, if any, children had rules that they were expected to follow at home; nor was there a stable and consistent family structure in place for them to model. Children were given the freedom to do and say whatever they wanted without a given script to rehearse or follow. What behavior was an unlearned and undisciplined child expected to model on his own?

New Family Model

Working parents are now the standard model of families today. Working parents remain actively involved in pursuing jobs, career development, and other areas of personal interests. The needs of the family and parenting their children remain the lesser priority. For this reason, many adult children carried over from their childhood into their adult lives unhealed wounds, hurts, unresolved bitterness and resentments from the past. America's landscape overflows with angry adults who were not raised by their biological parents caused by the shift in parental priorities. The lingering pain for adult children with parents who were too busy doing their thing to make time for them was the unspoken message, "I was not that important to you."

Why Are Children Outraged?

Decades of adult children carry unreleased resentment towards their parents because their grandparents, relatives, schools, government, community, and church sponsored social institutions had to step in and do their job. They struggle emotionally everyday with feelings of rejection and insecurity caused by the abandonment of their biological parents. Also, they face the psychological struggle in trying to reason and find answers for what they perceive as something they could have done wrong that would cause their biological parents not to want them. They are angered by having sensed throughout their lives that a part of them was missing, and the fact that they had not been successful in filling the void on their own. Many adult children today are still plagued by feeling unworthy or undeserving of their parents' time and attention. Instinctively children internalize and blame themselves as the reason for their parents' breakup that can affect their future sense of well-being. Is it reasonable why children today are characterized as failing to show sorrowful remorse for their wrong actions? Is it also understandable why children have such a high tenacity of willpower to rise up and kill their parents without having any sense of guilt or regret? The practice of outsourcing childcare for children has interrupted, prevented, and weakened the bonding process that naturally occurs between parents and their children when they are young is the only logical explanation for the violent behavior that is found in children. Children don't see a difference in how they relate to their parents from any other adult. How long can a prosperous and growing nation like America brace itself to handle and manage such an ever present massive recycling of broken and hurting people without changing the way that we currently are operating?

Outsourcing Childcare

The outsourcing of childcare is a mask and cover up for absent parents that serves as an alternative for the lack of parenting children which is a vital and missing component in today's culture. It is America's weakest links and contributors of the disintegration of the family. Also, outsourcing childcare does not erase the fact that children have stopped being parented and it is not a family or national priority. The lack of parenting shows up consistently in every aspect of children's lives and in society as a whole. It is a direct connection to the cause of social ills and mayhem that plagues society today. The unresolved conflict of family priorities over parent occupations was left lying on the table in the 1960s and is still dormant.

Outsourcing is one of the fastest growing social epidemics to strip families of their heritage and family legacies. It is the engine that fills our jails and overcrowds our prisons. It is the cause for the inclusion of children in the fastest growing incarceration rate in America ("Juvenile Incarceration", 2014). Suicide also is a by-product that is the third leading cause of death among teens and continues to rise ("Youth Suicide", 2015). The "hands off" approach to parenting justifies youth presence and involvement in gangs, criminal, and other violent activities that are among us today. It has fueled misguided young males to adopt the philosophy that to make a baby would make him a man? Young girls bought in by making pacts to intentionally get pregnant out of wedlock. It is futile thinking for society to expect different results in inappropriate child behaviors today while the repetitive cycle that is set in motion allows for the non-engagement of parents as an acceptable practice.

Silent Consent

We too, cannot continue to unconsciously give our silent consent to unwholesome and unproductive parenting (childrearing) practices. Our current lack of effective childrearing practices hinders our progress and thwarts our efforts to move forward as a nation. We cannot afford to walk down this darkened path and ignore the costly and deadly legacy that ineffective childrearing practices have created. We must become aroused and challenged once again as good Americans to use our collective voices and efforts in breaking the silence. We must also interrupt the cycle of despair and hopelessness in our family life that propels us further down this misguided course into infinite darkness. As a nation can we ask ourselves have we reached a level of maturity that we can now say with a clear voice that we missed the mark in the 1960s on the issue of family life? And, how missing this mark has negatively impacted other critical areas of our lives? Have we also neglected and failed to meet the spiritual and emotional needs of our children by not properly nurturing their innate qualities and attributes necessary to build up their capacity to become caring, loving, productive and responsible adults? Are we willing to allow our children to live in constant pain and despair without knowing the true meaning and purpose for their lives? Have they only been programmed to reproduce, inflict and bring more pain and suffering into the world? Are children aimlessly wandering today not knowing who they are and what they can become? Have we failed to give children what is to be expected in every human being? We must begin to seriously consider as a matter of the heart to think, rethink and think again that children's lives matter.

Technology The New Babysitter

The disintegration of the family is an open declaration that children are America's biggest losers. What hope did children of previous generations have as they lost their parents and watched their home life fall into pieces before their eyes? The disintegration of the family has caused great hurt and harm to befall children's ongoing well-being. The lives of children were swiftly endangered by adverse circumstances were coming from within their own immediate families and homes. Working families' internal dispute over family and occupational priorities was the engine that became the driver for all family decisions including the breakdown and breakup of the family. Occupation was the popular choice and the number one priority of families that increased the demand for more childcare alternatives outside of the home. Families were in the thralls of divorce and breakdowns. Desperate and hurting parents (1970s) turned to technology (i.e. television, video games, music videos, and movie tapes as entertainment) as their designated babysitters. With this decision came an excessive exposure of children to various uncensored media sources. Captive child audiences were aggressively targeted and became one of leading sources of revenues for America's businesses. Unsupervised children became the innocent victims of technology and over media exposure. American homes were soon

43

inundated with large television marketing campaigns.

Toy manufacturers became big business enterprises overnight. Using children "for profit" was the name of the game and the cash cow that consistently filled America's financial reservoirs. On the political side, America cashed in also through deregulations that allowed the vulnerability of unsupervised children to become overexposed by the media that placed them at high risk and in harm's way of perpetual advertisement strategies. Nonetheless, the reality remains that parents have the primary responsibility of parenting their children which cannot be completely outsourced to technology, learning institutions, sports programs, and any other childcare agencies or organizations. Active parental engagement and participation in the home is crucial to the quality of life for children. The need for parents to get back into the game of actively raising their children themselves remains an essential part of the American framework.

Transformation of Schools

Troubled families further searched for childcare by turning to the schools for assistance. Their request created an outbreak of misunderstanding and began a long struggle between the schools and the parents over the changing role of the family. The struggle between parents and educators over the care of children has lasted for decades. This unresolved struggle trickled down as more and more children were engaged as players in the conflict that has been a major contributor that turned school campuses into battlegrounds of dissension. The 1990s Columbine High School massacre was reflective of the depth of how children had internalized the parent-teacher-child conflict which had never been heard of or seen before in America. The youth used technology and copied movie scenes and actors as role models for their violent behavior. Massive killings preceded the Columbine massacre and subsequent school shootings have followed. Thereafter, the trend started for children killing and injuring their peers, parents, teachers, etc. and was added to America's landscape. Children who murder is now the new normal.

Children's abilities to use positive problem solving skills in creative ways have become skewed by troubled families through the implied suggestive teachings of what I call their media families. Desperate parents did not anticipate there would be a transference of violent behavior from using technology as their babysitters. Unsupervised children began modeling violent behaviors learned by observing their make believe media families and heroes. Children also learned to trust their tech babysitters because of their consistent availability, and the attention was focused on them. Innocent children turned to technology instead of their parents for answers to their problems and dilemmas. Children daily received a steady diet of glamorized family dysfunction, mass killing, crime, sex scandals, first-time sex TV and movie scenes, wild parties, substance abuse, gangs, stealing, lying, and violence that were shown as fun and lessons on how to be cool.

Family Roles vs. School Roles

The schools were targeted as a major resource for childcare assistance by desperate parents. Their requests went far beyond the range and scope of the traditional school services. The needs of broken families were rapidly spilling over into the school environment. The schools were at the center of social change for children and their families. The National Center for Juvenile Justice Fact Sheet reported between 1970 and 1996, the number of divorced persons had more than quadrupled from 4.3 million to 18.3 million. Single parent families were left without the additional financial, physical and emotional support derived from two parents living in the home. The growing need for childcare became confrontational when demanding parents daily bullied school officials who had crossed them in their attempts to get schools to help meet their child care needs.

The conflict between parents, teachers, and children continued to build. During the 1970s, 1980s and the early 1990s children were the victims of an ongoing crossfire between the conflicting views and disagreements between their parents in their daily home life. At the same time, they were in the middle of a brewing and developing conflict of interest between two of the most powerful and important influencers in a child's life—their parents and teachers. When children reached school age, traditionally parents transferred an equal amount of "trust and authority" onto the teacher outside of themselves. The teacher-child relationship was ranked second in importance to that of the parents. The teacher-child relationship was foundational for the child. The parent bestowed trust and confidence in the teacher's ability to love, care and provide the appropriate instruction and guidance for their children. Parents instructed their children to trust, obey, listen, and follow the teacher's rules; and ask for their help if a problem arose, or if somebody bothered them while they were at school. Children were not to disrupt the classroom for any reason.

The parents supported the teacher-child relationship by being active and available to participate in helping to ensure quality learning was achieved by their child. Parents were expected to provide a proper home environment for their child that would support and reinforce his learning experiences at school. Parents ensured that children got their proper rest, completed their homework assignments with them, ate nutritious meals and snacks, regularly attended school, received medical/dental services, and had a safe place to live.

The parent and teacher discussed and shared any problems in the home that would hinder or pose a threat to the child's learning at school. Parents and teachers worked as a team in getting conflicts resolved respectfully and positively.

New Relationships

As the rising conflict tarnished the relationship between families and schools continued, parents resorted to non-traditional ways and means of instructing their children. Parents out of fear of retaliation from the schools, began to teach their children how to scrutinize the teacher's conduct and motives by questioning their children. Questioning of this sort came from children of all age groups began to permeate the school environment. At the end of the school day children faced a barrage of questions from their apprehensive parents. "What did the teacher do or say to you today?" If parents did not approve of their children's answers, a likely comment would follow, "What is that teacher's problem?" The end result: Parents knowingly taught their children how to be confrontational and combative with their teachers relative to sensitive matters that would ordinarily be handled between adults.

New Communications

Additionally, positive communications between teachers and students was distorted by parents teaching children how to "talk back" (past practices labeled it "back talk" which was considered disrespectful behavior for children towards adults; to stand their ground, and act like adults. Children equipped with this change in behavior, began to repeat negative remarks that was made to them by their parents about their teachers boldly repeat to their teachers the negative remarks that were made to them by their parents about their teachers; and children were expected to carry out their parents instructions to stand their ground. Comments such as "My mama told me to tell you that you are not my parent, and I don't have to do or listen to what you have to say." School officials were confronted with these negative comments coming from the mouths of babes that made communications fragile and sensitive between the students and their teachers. In the home, the practice of using their children as weapons against each other in family disputes, and the same practice of using their children as weapons was also taken to the schools. Innocent children had become a part of the ongoing battle between adults.

Eye Witnesses

Children lost the stability and the security of a healthy home life with two parents who loved them and had become the victims of their parents' bitterness and brokenness. Simultaneously, children were facing the threatening loss of a quality teacher-child relationship as well. Children witnessed first-hand threats that were made by their parents to have their teachers fired.

Children also heard their parents' barrage of constant threats made to schools officials of their plans to go to the School Board of Education if that was what it took to get the results they wanted. Also, children heard the fire backs that came from the schools as well. Children while in their educational development were also in the middle of learning a valuable life lesson from hearing and by observing two of their most powerful and influential authority figures negatively handle conflict and opposing viewpoints. They were in the middle of a tug-of-war at home and at school with no control over either outcome.

Schools Regenerated

In an effort to assist parents with their child care needs, schools were required to shift in how they would operate in the future. Schools slowly began to incorporate many of the duties and responsibilities that were once held by parents. As the schools were transitioning into assuming some of the families former roles, parents assumed the role of parent advocates fighting for the rights of their children. This was a significant victory for single families in getting help with childcare were also fueled by the support of the Women's Rights Movement mainly to help mothers who were working, single mothers who were in school or enrolled in job training programs. The winning argument for requiring schools to broaden its base was that these mothers did not have the time to prepare meals and feed their children at home and get to work or class on time. To fill that need, schools instituted the breakfast program to feed the children.

Prior to the schools adjusting their operating hours, and before the breakfast program was incorporated as a part of the regular school day, while taking my child to school, I frequently witnessed parents who drove away with their children left behind on the school's doorsteps before school was scheduled to open. Children were left hungry, out in the rain and the cold because parents had to go to work or class and had no childcare resource. Teachers also found learning to be very difficult for these children because they could not focus or concentrate on their work because they were hungry. For the single parent, their new role as the primary breadwinner in the family caused them to take such risks in order for them to keep their jobs. Keeping a job became their number one priority out of necessity. This condition placed an insurmountable pressure on schools to change how they operated.

Additionally, schools were shifted to support families by providing afterschool care for children, snacks and tutorial services. Parents eagerly signed permission slips giving schools permission to teach sex education to their children. Schools provided nurseries to care for pregnant students unborn babies. Schools also began to provide care for sick children within the school setting. Nurses were hired and space was made available for the care of sick children. Traditionally, it was not permissible for parents to send sick children to school, nor was it permissible for schools to store, dispense or give children medications during school operating hours. It was the responsibility of the parent to provide the care for their sick child. Simply stated, parents' availability to their children became less and less regardless of the reason. What changes need to occur that again will make the needs of children America's number one priority now and in the future?"

Victimization of Children

Children's familiar school relationships and the overall school environment were vanishing. Their daily school routines had begun to resemble activities that were once shared in their homes with their immediate family members. Home life and school life were coming together in a way that would change the whole dynamics of how schools in the future would function and operate in America. How were the children prepared to handle these new experiences between the most powerful institutions in their lives that were simultaneously thrust upon them? The need for social change created the conditions that caused the lives of innocent children to become the victims of change.

Children as containers have carried the seeds that were planted in them by their broken homes and school relationships. What were the seeds of conflict between

52

the parents and schools that filled up the containers? How has the growth of the seeds impacted the containers? How much attention was given to the condition of the containers? Have the seedlings outgrown their original containers? Was unwanted plant growth removed from the containers as they grew? What signs tell us that the containers cracked carrying the weight of adult conflict?

Presently in America, the radical seeds of rebellion that were planted during the 1960s set the stage for traumatic conditions that children yet to be born would experience. Seeds of discord, anger, rejection, bitterness, resentment, retaliation, and depression were planted and watered daily by disgruntled adults over who would care for the children.

Generational Crisis

Children's loss of priority in the family, family disintegration, absentee parents, and broken teacher-child relationships are critical issues of the American culture. These issues have endangered generations of children who was, who is, who will be born with the loss of a positive spiritual inheritance, and uncertain of their authentic identities. Generations have been born carrying seeds of perpetual hate, prejudices and biases. Generations have been born carrying seeds of perpetual poverty, homelessness and family dysfunctions. Generations have been born addicted to drugs, alcohol and the HIV/AIDS virus. Generations have been born into perpetual crime, violence, shame, greed, fear, self-centeredness and hopelessness. Generations have been born unwanted, fatherless, neglected, abused and victims of human trafficking. Generations have been born to absentee parents. Generations have been nurtured by technology that trained them to be impersonal, uncaring, unable to problem solve, and be independent thinkers. Generations have been born to look for the easiest way to get ahead without regard or respect for the rights and fair treatment of others. Generations have been born having a destructive nature to cause perpetual harm to others without feeling remorse; and refusal of longstanding commitment to anybody or anything. Generations have been born that must confront the unthinkable—polluted air, water, land and insurmountable debt.

The containers (children) have brought to bear the seeds that were planted inside them. Will the practice of outsourcing childcare continue? Will parents become willing to adjust their time and priorities? Will a caring society reposition itself to promote, support and help to elevate the quality of life for the survival of future generations? Will America adjust its course in time?

CHAPTER FOUR

Raising Children In A Village Without Walls

America has reached an historical plateau where the value of the family and the quality of family living are at high risk. Modern day families are fragmented, and they are unconsciously attempting to raise their children in a culture that does not possess a life sustainable framework that is positive, and is without clearly defined commonly shared family values. The foundation of the family lacks sound moral and positive values upon which families can build and grow. Additionally, America's long neglected and long overlooked failure to address the critical issue of how children are raised has brought us to this crossroad of uncertainty in the very core of family life. The modern family's ability to influence and effectively raise happy, productive, and healthy children is prohibited by severe, adverse, and harsh environmental factors as well. Having this turbulent void in family life gives added velocity to the existing social chaos and damage that are also present in other social areas in America. Together, their unified potential is intensified and can cause greater social disharmony and disarray that society have ever known such as the non-existence of the human family.

For many of you reading this book, it is possible that you were born at a time when traditional family values and childrearing practices were transitioning or had already become obsolete by the majority of families. I will compare the present childrearing practices with the past by using the village concept that was once practiced in America. The village model conceptualizes and defines family values and childrearing practices; and it includes acceptable practices that the overall village used to build and support the quality and stabilization of the family. Also included are family legacies that were carried over from generation to generation.

All family values and practices that formed the basis of the traditional family were not an error as some thought. It was discovered that errors had been made in the interpretation of the scripture by the religious scholars. The sense of having too much structure, the 1960s youth "tossed the baby out with the bath water" by rejecting all organized religion and the family practices that were associated with them. Their decision to willfully reject all of the traditional family values and practices, caused a significant disruption in the continuity and quality of family life in America. This disturbed the overall structure of the home such as the lack of adherence to the rules of the family.

This disruption became reality when masses of children from middle and upper class families rebelled against the authority of their parents and elders. They refused to listen to what they had to say on critical subjects of interests. Also, the youth of the 1960s acted out their rebellion by changing their appearance and how they dressed; created and listened to music that had a different sound and message from that of their parents; became nonconformists of the status quo; and learned how to speak differently as well. Most notably this interruption in family life created a lasting disconnection between parents and children that have continued to our present day. This disconnection between parents and children is one of the chief reasons why America is experiencing such turbulence and unimaginable social crises. Child abandonment for the sake of personal pursuits has became a socially acceptable practice for parents today as a by-product of this breakdown in family relationships. As the years have gone by, this schism between children and their parents has taken an appalling toll on the present generation.

It Takes a Village to Raise a Child

The "village" concept for raising children was mainly peculiar to the African-American family and lifestyle. However, the majority of all American families shared similar common practices and values peculiar to them in varying degrees during a period in history when America was developing as a young and growing nation. In the village model, young parents respected the authority and wisdom of their parents and elders. They did this through their acknowledgement, acceptance and practice of the concept "it takes a village to raise a child", and willingly forfeited their right to parent their children exclusively on their own. They also understood and recognized their children as being a part of the ongoing legacy of the family.

Village Benefits

A key value in the village model as well was the support and benefits that was initiated and offered by the extended family at the onset of a pregnancy. The extended family showed their support by allowing newlywed couples to move in with them in order to help them to get a head start in life. It was not uncommon for young couples to get married and live at home with the husband or the wife's family until they had secured their own place and had accumulated enough finances to move out on their own. Of course these arrangements were made in advance with the extended family's approval prior to the couple actually moving into their home. Newlywed couples understood they were guests in their parents' homes for a designated period of time, and they were expected to respect and abide by their parents' house rules during their stay. Being an adult was irrelevant, following their rules is what mattered. Couples were never totally dependent on their parents (host family) to meet all of their basic needs and obligations. Young couples was expected to carry their own weight by helping to share financially in the overall operating household expenses (i.e. food purchases, assisting with household chores, gardening, etc.) while building up their nest egg to move out.

To show their appreciation, newlywed couples had a willingness to help support the host family in whatever way they could as an expression of their gratitude for allowing them to live in their home. For example, they might voluntarily do the host family's laundry for them or wash the dishes every night. Young couples also enjoyed the benefit of having their parents' wisdom and guidance ready and available to help them during times of emergencies. They had free childcare and support with their children. Also, their parents were accessible in helping them to make critical marital adjustments and handling daily dilemmas that were common to married life.

Extended Family Benefits

For young couples who were already married and out on their own, when the young wife became pregnant, weeks before her expected delivery date, the practice was to move in with her family to be near them. The extended family members would all share in helping to provide for her care and needs, while the expectant mother focused on preparations for the new baby's arrival. Extended family members and nearby neighbors also gave their support by assuming the duties of her household and family that she had left behind. During her absence they prepared and cooked the family's meals, washed, ironed the laundry, cleaned the house and assisted with other household chores as they were needed until the wife returned and was ready to resume her duties. The expectant mother's house ran smoothly by the family and neighbors as when she was present. Never was the kindness of the neighbors and family members taken for granted or taken advantage of by young couples. It was considered to be very disrespectful and unacceptable for couples to exhibit an unappreciative attitude for the kindness and love that had been shown to them, and such behavior was frowned upon by the elders.

Modern Family Practices

Grandparents are expected to accept their children's new roles and behaviors that they have defined for themselves without respect or regard for their person, property or possessions. It's all about them and what they want. Today's young married and unmarried families demand, expect and feel "entitled" to receive the benefits of the extended family without taking any responsibility for the welfare and upkeep of the total household. Grandparents are expected to provide free lodging for their married and unmarried children as needed with the added benefit of no responsibility for their own personal upkeep as well. The expectation is for their parents to continue their financial allowances to be used as their source of income. They expect to live in their parents' home without respecting their values, following the rules and practices of their home, and have the option to live and be treated as independents with the freedom to live separate from the extended family. Having a sense of giving back and being connected is foreign to them.

Additionally, active and caring grandparents are expected to be financially responsible (for their grandchildren), and to take the lead role in providing free and on demand childcare. Today's married and unmarried children's preference is to live as non-contributing family members in their parents' home without them having or showing any signs of their disapproval. They expect a free ride, demanding to be treated as adults while behaving like children. Open disrespect and the lack of gratitude are worn and shown by young couples as a badge of honor as repayment for the unmerited kindnesses shown to them by their parents

Conflicting Practices

Another benefit of family life in the village that young parents enjoyed was the privilege of taking their newborn to their extended family or a nearby neighbor's house when they became too exhausted as parents, and needed a break from the continuous care of their new baby. As expressions of their love and kindness, family members and neighbors welcomed and freely offered their help in taking care of the baby. Unlike today, young mothers are single and raising their children alone and in isolation. They lack the support that is derived from their extended family members and neighbors to help them to meet the needs and demands

61

of raising a child. Child abuse and neglect is the main result of such a tedious and ongoing task for the young single mother. Also, within the village (neighborhood or community) no family or child could ever find themselves without the love, support and protection of the entire village. A first time pregnancy out-of-wedlock act was pardonable, yet the behavior was not expected to be repeated. Young or old, parents were expected to raise their children with the support of the immediate family and village.

The village culture was for villagers to rally, support and to help meet the needs of each other. Everyone was expected to govern themselves by upholding the shared common values and practices of the village. Village support would be given to any villager who became ill, out of work, or fell on hard times. Unlike today, generosity is shown when there is an emergency or a terrible disaster. In the past, villagers mainly worked for themselves and grew their own food. The common practice was to share their harvest with each other. As a child growing up, I can recall seeing people in my neighborhood picking-up and dropping-off food from house to house. My grandmother had me deliver food from her garden to the neighbors' house, and I frequently went along with my friends when they had to deliver food as well. No one ever went hungry because sharing with others was their way of life, unlike today where there is an overabundance of food, and yet people are hungry. Likewise, no one was without a place to live because villagers always made room even if the space for sleeping was the floor in their home.   Yet, today people are homeless and there are numerous vacant spaces where people could be sheltered. Loving your neighbor as yourself was the common value and quality of life in the village.

The Heart of the Villager

The hearts of the villagers of the past were more loving and receptive to meeting the needs of others whereas, the hearts of today's villagers are more open to meeting their own selfish needs. In the past, neighbors were at liberty to borrow a cup of sugar or milk from each other if they ran out of the ingredient while they were in the midst of preparing a meal. There was no need to get in your car and drive to the nearby food market and pay twice the cost for the item when your neighbor was next door. Villagers could leave their doors unlocked while they slept with the windows open without the threat of being physically harmed or the loss of possessions. Unsecured toys, equipment, clothing, unlocked parked cars, and food growing in nearby gardens describe the quality of life in the village. If prewashed laundry was left hanging outside on the clothes lines and a sudden rain came up while the family was not at home, a nearby neighbor would remove the clothes from the clothes lines so they would not get wet and would later return the dry laundry to the family.

Village Childcare Practices

Provided by the village, free childcare for all children—
not just for newborns only was another valuable practice
that helped to strengthen families by the village. A
mother could run short errands and leave her children
outside in the family's yard to play. She could ask her
neighbor from across the street to keep an eye on them
while she was away. The neighbors gladly helped each
other in this way with caring for the children. The
children however, were expected to stay in the yard as
they had been told. The children understood that it was
not an option whether or not they were to obey the
neighbor. They knew if they did not obey their mother's
instructions, the neighbor had already been given
permission by their mother to discipline them in her
absence. Children's failure to follow their mother's
instructions would result in immediate on-the-spot
discipline executed by the neighbor. Follow-up and
additional disciplinary actions by the parents would be
made at home for their failure to do as they had been
"told". The word of the parent had final authority in the
lives of all children. The parents' word was always
enforced and given additional strength by supportive
family and members of the entire village as well. This
was a true demonstration of what respect for all
authority figures looked like for children. They knew
and understood they were under the protection and
supervision of adult figures at all times until they

became of age to be on their own.

Parents As Role Models

Parents strongly believed they were directly responsible
for showing and teaching their children the value of
knowing the right way to live, and how to get along
with others. Religion and parents walked hand- in-hand
in governing the affairs and guiding the directions that
children should take in life. Parents took the job of
raising their children seriously. For this reason, they
made sincere and constant efforts to parents to their
children. Unlike today, the parent-child relationship is
to be their child's friend. Children primarily learned by
following their parents' example of how they should
behave, show respect for their elders, and to know right
from wrong. Inappropriate behavior by children
towards adult figures simply was not tolerated—no
matter the given circumstance. Parents did not fear
disciplining their children to correct their bad behavior.

Loving Your Neighbor as Yourself

Neighbors were expected to treat and care for all
children in the village as if they were their own. There
was no partiality and unfair treatment given to children.
If a child was at a neighbor's home and it was dinner
time, the child ate dinner with the neighbor. It would
have been considered rude and disrespectful for the child
not to eat. Eating at a neighbor's house was considered
a friendly and hospitable practice of endearment in the

African American culture where food was often very scarce—your family was my family.

If the parents were away on family business for a long period of time during the day, the children could be taken to a neighbor who would care for them at no cost. The outcome of this shared practice was to return the favor, or show your appreciation for their kindness in some other meaningful way. Money was seldom used to show appreciation for shown kindnesses. Money offered for repayment would be turned down by the villagers. Practicing the universal principles of faith and trust in your neighbor was the main currency of village life. Helping your neighbor was seen as a privilege and opportunity to do random acts of kindness. For example, if a neighbor was a mechanic and your car needed repairs, the neighbor repaired the car at no cost to the neighbor in need.

Shared Values

The commonly shared universal values and practices were the bond that helped to form the invisible walls that were not made by human hands. The practice and use of these principles was applied in the villagers daily lives. By living these changeless principles, the "people" themselves were the "living invisible walls" that provided the love, trust, warmth, security, and the protection of the community against adversarial forces. For this reason alone, families had the capacity to sleep with unlocked doors and open windows without fear of his neighbors, because neighbors in deed practiced being their brothers' keeper. The people treated their neighbors as they would like to be treated.

Children learned valuable life lessons from within the village. Consistency inside the village helped children to build strong character and positive values, and at the same time helped to strengthen their personal family relationships. Neighbors did not cross over the established boundary lines and values of the immediate family, but rather supported and helped to strengthen the family. Community support is key to the family's ability to be strong and successful. The job of being a parent was backed by a strong community. The quality of family life was conducive and sustaining for ongoing generations.

A Weakened Family Base

Unlike the village concept of family life, today's families are characterized by hurting, wounding and even killing their parents and relatives. Bullying in families (and neighborhoods) is a widespread common practice of the modern day. In the village, parents were expected to actively function and be available for their children. Parents could be trusted to do the right thing for their children in meeting their physical, educational, emotional, social, mental and spiritual needs. Today, families are operating under an open window that believes it is up to the individual to do what they want to do.

Therefore, no boundaries have been set, and families do not have a commonly shared framework in place to help guide family interactions and behaviors. There is no framework for parents and children that will help and teach them how to control and guide their actions towards each other; and that will ensure the overall good of others as well. Also, families today lack a shared vision and common purpose for the overall direction of the family. Families today are producers of mass murderers, thieves, selfishness, greed, sexual predators, hatred of others, impoverished people, homelessness, fatherlessness, materialism, etc.

Village Without Walls

As the need for social reform became the main priority in the 1960s, America as a nation began shifting and changing its direction and path as a result of the unprecedented pressures and demands for government intervention by its citizenry grew stronger. The concept of village life under the old practices "systematically" began to be phased out as the new village began to emerge. What remains of the old village today? What are the new fundamental values and virtues that the new village is founded upon? Is the quality of family life better as envisioned by the 1960s? What are the new and innovative childrearing practices that have replaced the old? How have the lives of children improved?

I refer to the new village concept of family life and childrearing practices in America today as parenting in a "village without walls". The village without walls concept is based on the carried over mind-set and philosophy of the 1960s, "If it feels good do it." With freedom as the currency, everyone was free to do their own thing with little or no regard for the differing values and opinions of others. "You do your thing, and I will do my thing" is still around to the present day.

In the 1960s to be different and radical was considered cool and everyone wanted to be cool. When this phase ended, the press for personal ambition, status, success and greed began to surface. More and more of the old village principles and way of life were fading away as the "new way" was pressing forward.

The new wave of the 1960s was thrust into the 1970s and the 1980s; and coupled together, these decades took the philosophy of the 1960s to another level. Also, young radicals heavily armed with a new philosophy of their own, "What's in it for me?" with an added mixture of "Me- Me- Me" all three successfully went mainstream into the American experience. These ideologies encapsulated the new culture's way of doing things. The 1980s primary preoccupation was partying, designer labels, education, status and success. "Greed is good" was the flavoring that fueled personal drive and the ambition to succeed at any cost. Massive spending and credit card debt became the new standard of living for families in the new village. The bases of the new standards were grounded in doing what was in the best interest of the individual, and not what was in the best interest of the people. The individual's right to choose and be governed by their own self-defined standards of right and wrong, good and bad was the acceptable path to follow. The new villagers moved aggressively in exiting the old village way of living in favor of the new.

As village practices were being outdated, finding safety and protection became a constant and growing challenge because villagers now lived in fear of their neighbors. Villagers today do not know who their neighbors are by name, and live isolated from each other. Villagers have abandoned the practice of being their brothers' keeper. The new practice is "every man is for himself" and "if you snooze you lose". Safety and protection of children is self-governed by the children themselves who formed and joined gangs in spite of their parents' objections and society's fears and disapproval. Villages now require man- made walls and systems to be built for safety and protection "from" his neighbor. Also, village safety and protection has been reduced to security cameras, burglar bars, alarm systems, and gated communities which are subject to breakdowns, wear out, damage, faulty equipment, replacement and ongoing repairs. Today's villagers sleep and live behind locked doors, windows and high tech security systems for their personal safety as a means of protecting themselves, possessions, and their property. The new villagers normally do not cross over boundary lines to help assist each other. If a neighbor today telephones the police when someone's home is being burglarized while they are not at home, the neighbor who telephones the police is considered a hero for their kind gesture. Payment for the neighbor's act of kindness is a televised interview which is aired on the evening news. The common practice; however, is for each neighbor to have his own security alarm system, and it is the responsibility of the security alarm company to place the call to the police.

Financial progress, education achievements, ongoing advancements in technology designed to help improve the quality of life, helped the old values and virtues to slip away. They no longer held the same place of value and relevancy in the new way of living. Adopting new ideologies guided by the new perceptions "To each his own" and "you got yours, and I got mine" now were the commonly shared values and acceptable practices of the new village. What is the fate of villagers who are not high achievers and cannot make it on their own? Financial empowerment; however, gave new villagers the means to become more independent, and less dependent on the extended family and villagers for support and assistance.

Successful new families chose to live exclusively on their own by accepting full responsibility for the handling and the upkeep of their homes, and the care of their newborn children. New jobs would often relocate the new families far away from their immediate families and familiar surroundings. With the distance, adherence to old family legacies automatically was challenged and disrupted. Couples followed their careers and job opportunities and were willing to relocate their families to accept the offer of the highest bidder. Paid childcare and jobs with maternity leave benefits enabled young villagers to become more self-sufficient as well. Grandparents were now invited to come and assist the young family within the comfort and privacy of their own home with their new baby. They would also be in charge of their home and live by their own set of rules. New parents now were afforded the opportunity to parent their children in their own way, according to their set of values, and different lifestyles.

Parenting Challenges

Nonetheless, young couples were not without struggles and challenges of their own as parents in raising their children. In difficult times, they felt alone and longed for the support of the extended family they had earlier rejected. Their challenge were inappropriate behaviors in their children that were never seen or heard of when they were children. Young families were without a point of reference on how to handle the growing challenging behaviors of their children which have become an ongoing problem. Families confronted with new and different parenting challenges require newly creative, innovative ways and means of setting, determining, and achieving parenting goals for children that will correct inappropriate behaviors.

A main factor to consider is the composition of today's new village that is mainly comprised of working class families who can only exercise limited parental authority and control over their children. Work restrictions prohibits working parents effectiveness as parents due to inadequate time off from their jobs that would allow their direct involvement and participation in their children's daily lives and activities. Ongoing job opportunities and career success has created the development of chronic absentee parents. The lack of parenting children is a major breakdown in the family's ability to achieve and maintain the quality of family life that growing families need to successfully thrive. With absentee parents has come the loss of the parent's word to effectively influence children's behavior. In the past, the parent's word carried authority; but the parent's word no longer has the final say in a child's life today. Heavy and unrelenting work pressures and demands diminish the parent's capacity and high energy levels that are required to enforce their spoken word as well as to keep a watchful eye on their children.

Alternative Childcare

Paid childcare replaced the watchful eye of the next door neighbor who watched out and cared for all of the village children. Children are left to their own self-care today if parents are unable to pay for childcare, and if community resources are limited. Through paid community activities such as sports programs, children are able to gain access to positive non-parental adult authority figures to build positive relationships. Neighborhood Watch programs were instituted to assist communities, but due to the frequency of families' transitioning from neighborhood to neighborhood, maintaining their effectiveness is very challenging.

Ineffective Parenting Practices

Weak and ineffective parenting strategies placed children at high risk for exhibiting inappropriate behaviors that challenged the authority of adult figures. One harmful strategy created and used by working parents was to teach their offspring language that was inappropriate for children and was primarily used by adults only. Children were taught how to address and respond inappropriately to non-parental adults such as their teachers, and called it "being assertive" when in reality they were taught how to be disrespectful. This practice misaligned children with society and caused the creation of new laws and modifications of the existing laws to govern children's behavior. New societal perspectives and new laws changed the way children were viewed and treated in America for their misconduct. This serious misalignment of children that was caused by their parents is responsible for the introduction and institution of the new laws for when children behave like adults, they would also be treated and penalized in the same way as if they were in fact adults.

Schools and the communities were confronted with the new, different and difficult challenging behaviors in children that had begun to spin far beyond their scope and ability to control. The schools' discipline methods, policies and procedures were not effective in controlling children's challenging behaviors in the classroom and in the overall school environment. Parents stood in opposition to, rather than in agreement with, community leaders over the distressing issues relative to how children should be disciplined. Parents also were uncertain and at a loss of how and what needed to be done to correct the growing and challenging behaviors in their children. Unfortunate for the children, parents opposed the schools' established rules for handling student misconduct, and resorted to denying that the bad behavior existed. Instead, parents rewarded their children's wrong behavior as their means of discipline. This is yet another misguided parenting practice that has laid a shaky foundation towards building America's new family model. The practice of rewarding negative behavior interrupts and undermines the natural occurrence of consequence that follow bad behavior and bad decisions. Nature is then prevented from having its role in helping to teach and instill positive values. With this practice, the capacity for children to make good decisions becomes jaded, and their wrong behavior goes uncorrected. It is also a precursor that has set up a platform for the high incarceration rate of children as well. The institution of these new practices was a clear indication that the ways of the old village were crumbling down all around us, and being replaced with new ones that did not promote, build up or develop strong character, values and integrity in children for future generations.

With the new set of values and concepts being taught by parents, children were given the latitude to freely make bad decisions and to exude bad behavior without having the foreknowledge of what it would later cost them and the rest of society. Also, under this practice children soon were able to realize that there were no anticipated consequences that would be forthcoming from their parents. Their attitudes reflected the false assumption that if their parents had no objections to what they did or said, the opinions of others were irrelevant and worthy to be disregarded. As a reminder, the family is the base and support system upon which our nation is able to stand and be effective. The family is the unit and fabric that builds, shapes and molds the character, integrity, respect, dignity and lifts up sound values that help to make America strong.

Foundational Pillar Shaken

Prior to the 1960s, parents were the designated people in America whose primary responsibility was to raise children who would grow up and become productive citizens. The role as disciplinarian of their children was one of the key duties and responsibilities of a parent that have been forfeited and neglected. Also, parents are lacking in fulfilling their responsibility to teach and execute the true value and meaning of allowing consequences to correct wrong behavior in children. Parents have bypassed taking corrective disciplinary actions themselves and instead have passed it along to community leaders for enforcement which has caused great conflict and hardship for everyone. Their neglect in fulfilling their parental duties in this area further placed community leaders in harm's way. Principals, teachers and police officers have been injured and even killed by undisciplined children. Entire communities have been burglarized and terrorized by children as well. In this consciousness, generations of children have been born who show no regard or have any fear of consequences no matter the outcome. Parents once upon a time could use telling the teacher or use the threat of going to jail as a fear tactic to deter wrong behavior in their children. In today's culture that fear tactic has no bearing on children's behavior at all. This new village practice alone, has provided a lasting, damaging, and dangerous impact on one of our nation's most critical foundational pillars which is the family. We can no longer ask ourselves how America's children got this way.

Seeds of Corruption

The corruptive seeds of the 1960s that were planted, changed the way America's children are parented. These corruptive seeds are now being harvested and lived out in our present culture. The 1960s strategy to change how future generations of children would be parented was effectively set in motion during the 1970s and 1980s when the "us mindset" was replaced with a "me mindset." The new generation of families objected to anyone guiding and looking over their shoulders. With the traditional way of parenting children being eliminated from America's equation for success, undisciplined children rapidly became a menace to society. The authority of the village was stripped as the continuous political and legal actions of parents that rendered it ineffective and inoperable. In this new environment, children became open prey for villagers having sinister motives. Life with sinister villagers living inside the village rapidly became the new normal. Instead of protecting and helping to keep children safe, they used their knowledge of parental absenteeism to employ their unthinkable, selfish and cunning wiles against children. The village that once helped to protect children and to keep them safe out of harm's way was gone. The village without walls was under siege by undisciplined and unruly villagers who created all kinds of social mayhem.

Parenting With A Focus

As parents became more and more distracted by heavy and untimely demands placed upon them by their jobs, careers, businesses and personal ambitions to achieve success, parenting children was substituted with many things. Parents were more interested in giving their children things they never had as children. They also wanted to provide them with more opportunities to become more successful. Parents main priority focused on growing the successful child athlete, musician and celebrity. The power of things, possessions, achievements and making money took control. The value of parents nurturing the development of the child's innate qualities and virtues fell by the wayside.

A major consequence of the new parenting strategies is now over four decades of children who have never been parented by their biological parents. Was it the vision and intention of the 1960s to do away with parenting children entirely? Or, has a serious error been made? Work and occupation are the driving forces that determine family values, not what is in the best interest of children. The family's needs now center around the needs and best interests of their careers and job opportunities. In the absence of parents spending quality time with their family, children more and more become the beneficiaries of their parents' material wealth. Why wouldn't the interests of children reflect the same interests of their parents? In the modern family, the ability to make money is highly valued and is used as a powerful tool for building the acquisition of things. Providing children with material goods and means is the acceptable way of life. However, using these methods has not corrected children's disruptive and inappropriate behaviors.

The Unknown Villager

The villager is unknown today and is the greatest threat and cause of crime and harm in the "village without walls." The new village is filled with strangers coming and going freely. No one shows real concern for the other but keep to themselves. The village resembles fragmented and broken families that are scattered about chanting their new mantras. The village is contaminated and endangered by villagers who cannot be trusted. The ability to trust each other was the glue of the past that held and sustained the quality of life in the village. The lack of trust among villagers is responsible for the decay and rotting away of the village. With the lack of trust gone, the new villagers are operating without a sustainable family foundation and defense upon which families can build and grow.

Villagers do not have a "watchful eye" for the village or villagers. Instead, they look the other way. Man-made security replaced trusting the neighbor, and is the alternative system that is now used. Man-made defenses; however, are no match for the trust and watchful eye of a caring neighbor.

New villagers live in constant fear caused by the uncertainty of not knowing who can and cannot be trusted. The loss of trust has developed unpredictable behaviors in the villagers that are unwholesome and threaten the capacity of the village to adequately sustain itself. Service persons who enters the home, office and business are often the same people who will later rob and steal back the items within the homes and businesses they service. The villager who delivers and steals from you is one and the same. Villagers expect to be robbed and cheated by their fellow villagers, this is the new normal for village life. As children are born, this is the environment that they find and adapt to as their way of life. There is no other history for them. The lack of trust is a widespread behavior in America. If workers are having a bad day or are angry at a supervisor, the outlet for the unhappy worker is to place a defective part on the car of an innocent customer. There are far too many accidents that has been contributed to faulty parts and repairs. It does not matter to the worker that it could cause potential harm and death to others. Villagers have no way of knowing for sure who can be trusted to do the right thing. The minister, parent, teacher, police officer and the coach all symbolize villagers of the past who could once be trusted. Now they have become unrecognizable threats who have taken on new and hidden identities that are beneath these images that cannot be easily discerned.

Many political leaders are more concerned with their own special interests and not in the interests of the people they serve. They have become leaders of corruption that is influenced by greed, bias and hatred of their neighbors. The point that I am making on why trust is so important is the fact that if the people who are preparing the food, operating the machinery, driving the bus, operating the computer, repairing the car, and defending you in court are all untrustworthy; we all are in trouble. The unthinkable can happen, which we are now experiencing. Untrustworthiness is the chief hidden and invisible culprit that is preventing and destroying our efforts to living quality lives.

Quality living cannot be realized when villagers have to watch their backs out of fear and uncertainty about the intentions and integrity of their neighbor.

Village Life for Children

Are children today justified in their bad behavior when they are over exposed to a way of life in the new village where the sensual behaviors and deviant appetites of adults run rampant throughout the village? Can you imagine America repeating the practice of slavery in the 21st century? The village is filled with drugs and alcohol abuse that is unsafe and unhealthy for children to live. Children can see villagers addicted to these substances trying to escape the realities of life. Adult villagers recruit and introduce children to a way of life that is filled with crime and violence. There is no need for children to stray when everything is within their reach to live an unproductive life. Children can easily find avenues within their reach to live unproductive lives within their homes, schools, and communities. The landscape is overcrowded with conditions of fatherlessness, hopelessness, single parent households, homelessness, drug dependency, etc. Is it justifiable that children turned to each other and formed gangs to provide for their own care, safety, and protection?

How can America continue to grow and build as a prosperous nation when its chief foundational pillar(the family) has lost its course and direction? How can the American family hope to survive this self-inflicted family holocaust? Today, families appear to be numbed to the present realities that children are destined to face when they are born into an environment that lessens their chances of survival. From birth their lives will inevitably be challenged by a myriad of fear, turbulence, and unpredictable recurring social issues that will place them constantly place them at high risk. With collapsed family walls of the past, and the new walls greatly flawed, raising children in this toxic environment presents tremendous hardships and disadvantages to effectively parent and children. This is a major factor new families must carefully consider. How will modern families prioritize the parenting of their children relative to what toxic social issues they will address first? Teach their children how to avoid contracting the AIDS virus? How to avoid becoming a drug dealer or human slave trafficker? Would it be teaching them how to properly use an oxygen mask because of air pollution? Would it be how to recognize the dangers of terrorism? Or, how to teach them to know who can be trusted when something is wrong? Regrettably, this is what family life in America has come to.

America must become aggressive in restoring the institution of the family and its place of value and worth in its overall framework. Families must be infused with a renewed sense of purpose and commitment to rebuilding the family on a solid foundation that has sound and universal values that everyone can live by.

Chapter Five

WHY DID WOMANHOOD CHALLENGE MOTHERHOOD?

Until the late sixties, the concept of motherhood carried with it a natural expectation that was gender based. It was the common belief of the family and society that the primary role of women was to conceive, carry, birth, and provide the ongoing care and nurturing of the family's offspring. Over the last four decades the concept of motherhood was challenged and has evolved. It is objectively viewed today as an unnatural expectation for women to be the primary caregivers of their children. Motherhood is now termed "parenthood" which means that males and females are the primary caregivers of their children. However, there are certain attributes that women have that are compatible and specific to the role of mothers:

- Motherhood is to assist the Creator by aiding in the nurturing and development of the divine attributes within children.
- Motherhood is a bond of trust that is given to women by God for the ongoing reproduction of humankind.
- Motherhood is a joint venture between God, the mother and her offspring.

- Motherhood models the innate bond of trust that exists between women and the Creator onto their offspring.
- Motherhood ensures that children receive the time and attention necessary for their successful spiritual, physical, emotional and cognitive development.
- Motherhood nurtures innateness.
- Motherhood is an assignment.
- Motherhood ensures the bond of trust between a mother and her child is the first life experience that her children receives.
- Motherhood ensures that children are not abandoned to care for their own needs prematurely.
- Motherhood ensures the laying a solid foundation within children based on sound values that will anchor and sustain the ongoing quality of life.

Changing Climate

As mothers were transitioning into the job markets, etc., I noticed changing behaviors in children that concerned me. Out of my love and compassion for children, I began my research to find answers that would explain why suddenly children in America were becoming outraged. As well as I wanted to know why they were openly displaying defiant, disrespectful attitudes and behaviors toward authority figures (i.e. parents, teachers, police officers). I further wanted to know what were the causes of their negative behaviors. These behaviors were only present in children from middle and upper middle families, but were now infiltrating mainstream America.

To explain children's behavior when they are acting out, I began first by taking a look at their parents, children's upbringing, and their environment. Also, as I considered the current plight of children that I was witnessing, I began to reflect on how I was raised. I noted there were considerable differences between the traditional and non-traditional family values and child rearing practices. The challenging behaviors in children that was emerging, questioned my personal beliefs about how children should be parented. I found that in both practices there were positive and negative values and outcomes. If an examination of the undesirable practices was initiated and the best of both practices were introduced, families today would have a model that would help them to successfully meet the present needs and demands of their children.

I targeted the mothers in looking to find reasons for the problems with our troubled youth. I completed high school in 1964. After marriage, divorce, and a single mother of six children, I made a hard and sacrificial decision <u>not</u> to reenter the work force which the working Mom was the fastest growing trend, while they were very young. I put my future and career plans on hold. I decided against joining the popularity of the status quo and not place my children in childcare. Instead, I remained at home with them. I agree with the definition of mother-hood as an assignment. During each of my pregnancies, I too sensed a strong bond of trust that was developing between God and me; once I had accepted the full responsibility of raising my children. Like the courts summons you as a potential juror to lay aside all other business to fulfill your civic duty to serve as a juror, I too sensed a calling in my heart that asked me to lay aside all of my business plans to fulfill my duty as a parent to serve as the mother of my children. I thought to myself what better way to develop into becoming a better person than by being an example for your children. I saw it as an opportunity for me to grow as an individual as they were growing.

The Search for Understanding

As I pondered and thought about my own personal experiences, I also thought about the rigorous ongoing care that children require and need from their mothers during children's early years. I entertained and questioned in my mind: (1)What would cause a woman to consciously challenge the male leadership in her home? (2) What would cause a woman to challenge her role; confront common beliefs and practices held by mothers; challenge family expectations; beliefs of the church, and society? (3) Most importantly, what would cause a mother to consciously risk placing the care of her children in the hands of total strangers?" I needed to know, What was driving the energy that had aroused women and caused them to knowingly set on fire their homes with the possibility of destroying their family as well? Coming from my own basic instincts as a woman and mother, these unanswered questions gripped my conscience to find the answer. Also, I needed to understand how America got to this place with our children and in our relationships.

Valley of Decision

As we all know, the basic instincts of a mother is to defend and protect her children at any cost. A caring mother would not deliberately and intentionally bring unnecessary harm to her children and family. For mothers to risk losing it all, the issue went much deeper than the fight to be freed from a gender based caste system of male dominance. In my attempts to find a logical reasonable explanation and motive, and to understand why mothers would consider in the first place to take on such a drastic undertaking. I explored the main probable cause that could be the energy behind the scene that was responsible for driving their decisions and actions. The Women's Rights Movement was initiated in the 1960s for women to obtain their human rights. In this movement women struggled to evolve as individuals by challenging the status quo of their day. Women desired the freedom to pursue their goals and dreams, find personal fulfillment, to be a participant in society, and to be productive in all areas of their lives.

They faced the hard choice of whether to realize and fulfill their own destiny, or to remain lost in subservient roles that offered controlled and limited possibilities. The decision whether to continue to follow or not to follow traditional concepts and ideas of women and mothers weighed in the balance.

Consultation

Briefly, let us go a little deeper and examine the findings and observations made by Erik Erikson a leading child psychologist. His theory gives us an explanation of the negative results that can occur during the period of early childhood when proper development is not successful.

(1) In children 0-18 months if basic trust is unsuccessful—a sense of mistrust develops.

(2) In children between the ages of 1-3 if autonomy does not successfully develop—shame is the outgrowth.

(3) In children during preschool ages 3-6 if denied opportunities to expand their self-initiative—guilt is formed.

(4) In school age children 6-11 are aware of their own self-worth and they make comparisons to that of their peers, if this stage in their development is not successful—inferiority forms and they will doubt their abilities to become successful.

(5) In adolescents ages 12-18, if a sense of self and self-identity is unsuccessful—leads to role confusion in their development, they question who they are, where do they fit and where are they going in life?(Falsetti, 2010)

Having this advantage by assuming that Erikson's theory is correct, it is then highly conceivable that traditionally women when they were little girls unsuccessfully went through the ages and stages of their childhood as undeveloped children. We can also safely say that when children are not given the proper nurturing during the early ages and stages of their growth and development, the logical outcome is for them to grow up lacking the necessary competency skills for them to become responsible and mature adults.

Male Caste System Explored

Under a male dominance system, the role that women were assigned to play in the home and in society was decided the day that a little girl was born. Having this disadvantage, the inevitable had to eventually occur— the liberation of women. Little girls were taught how to become subservient to others which is not a natural innate quality or trait that comes from within. However, from birth little girls were seen and treated as the lesser important member of the family and society. According to Erikson, it is during the early stages where successful childhood experiences such as learning basic trust, autonomy, initiative and competence are nurtured and developed. Little girls were denied their basic childhood experiences to explore and assert control over their physical bodies and environment. The denial of these basic childhood experiences developed within little girls feelings of inferiority, and a sense of dependency on others rather than independence that was being controlled by external factors.

The Answer Discovered

Erikson's theory gives us the understanding of "why womanhood challenged motherhood?" Generations of women denied their human rights and freedom had now grown up with unmet developmental needs from their childhood that began to rise up from within. The Women's Rights Movement was the vehicle that gave women a collective voice to cry out and the willingness to fight to be free from their oppression. Since childhood, the "woman" that was being held captive under the trappings of the role and standards of traditional motherhood had to stand up and be recognized for who she was, the gifts she possessed, and to take her assigned place in the world. Women's innate traits and attributes that were held down under the heavy weights of systemic male oppression had to be released regardless of the cost. As I said before, why would a mother consciously decide to jeopardize losing her relationships and family if the cause was not great enough.

Breaking Ties

Motherhood was much bigger than what it was thought and imagined to be. What could be a more propelling and driving force for women than to craft an internal shifting from what they were taught to be, in order to become who they were meant to become. The traditional female harness that had held motherhood in place was no longer pliable enough to bind and control the pressures that birthing womanhood required. Women had boldly and courageously risked losing it all in order to regain what had been lost to them as children, simply because they were born female. Womanhood triumphed and became the victor over the traditional concept of motherhood.

Soaring New Heights

Opportunities that were once denied to women became the spring board that launched women into a myriad of activities. Many ongoing efforts to dismantle the traditional roles that women once held were underway. Single and married women in record numbers bombarded the labor force, job training programs and enrolled in schools of higher learning as well. America was on the move. Women plunged forward to discover and gain their self-identity, to explore, establish and foster a sense of competency and pride in their abilities and accomplishments. The "woman" was finding her place, and discovering how high she could fly now that she was free from the controlling and oppressive limitations of her past. The false image and identity that had been assigned to women began to fade so that the true identity and self image of the authentic woman could appear.

Womanhood Emerges

Women went on to do exceptionally well in pursuing their careers and reaching their goals and dreams. Women in varying degrees enjoyed experiencing the autonomy of continuing to break down gender walls throughout every industry and profession. The new liberated woman was able to build her self-esteem and self-confidence in her abilities that had been oppressed. The nineties were marked as the decade of women in leadership by Time Almanac 2006 year- end report. To be a leader in business in the nineties was no longer an advantage to have been socialized as a man.

- Women increased in business and other professions from a minority of 10% in 1970 ranging from 30% to 50%.
- Men and women were on equal playing fields in corporate America.
- Since 1972 the percentage of women physicians doubled.
- 20% percent of all doctors and lawyers are women.

- Women hold 39.3% of the 14.2 million executive, administrative and management jobs (doubled since 1972—Bureau of Labor Statistics)
- Women accountants in 1972 rose from 21.7% to 49.6%.
- 83% female officers held titles of Vice-Presidents and better in Fortune 500 companies.
- 33% of women received MBA Degrees an increase from 11.7% in 1975.
- Women earned 13 times more engineering degrees since 1975 (American Association of Engineering Society).
- 44% adult working women are college educated increased from 20% in 1965.
- 84% of working women are part of the information service sector.
- Women started new businesses 2 times as fast as men.
- Working Women Magazine circulation grew from 450,000 copies in 1981 to 900,000 in 1988 -9.

Enlightenment

Because of the emergence of women we can recognize immediately the errors that were contained in the male caste system. It more evident than ever before that women are achievers. It has also been proven that a woman's value and worth had been misdiagnosed and misaligned. Under the practice of male dominance it was believed and practiced that women did not have the capacity to do anything other than homemaking and childrearing. This ideology denied women the right to be human and equal. A woman's husband had the final word on any matter. Men were exclusively the head of the household and could rule it in any way that they chose. A woman was expected to abide by and follow the rules of her husband. This defected belief and ideology was supported by the church and society. A woman's role was to please her husband. Women could be beaten and abused by their husbands and it was acceptable. Women submitted to their husbands out of the fear of retaliation. America is yet struggling today with this issue of men assaulting women. The husband controlled the finances; women were given allowances. The husband had the liberty to withhold spending privileges from his wife if she failed to please him. I remember a time when women were not allowed to open a banking account or get a credit card on their own without their husband's consent. Women had to pinch pennies in order to buy things for themselves and their children, and to give offerings to the church.

A woman was considered to be a good wife if she obediently followed her husband's leadership and decisions, whether he was a good leader or not. It was irrelevant whether the wife could handle certain tasks better than the husband. In many instances, the family suffered loss and harm which perhaps could have been avoided if the male leadership had been more flexible. Additionally, there were unjust, unfair laws, and practices that oppressed and held women in bondage to men. Women felt alone and entrapped in their own homes. Within this framework of family life, women suffered in silence.

Gender Based Childrearing

Growing up as children in America, boys and girls were reared based on gender biases and prejudices. Little girls were reared to be inferior to boys and men. Little girls were not given equal educational opportunities as little boys. Little girls were persuaded to pursue career opportunities in the helping professions as nurses, secretaries, flight attendants and school teachers. While little boys were given opportunities to become doctors, lawyers, engineers, pilots, business owners, etc. Boys were reared to believe their primary responsibility was to be the breadwinner of the family; and therefore, they needed higher incomes in order to support their families. Additionally, the image for little boys was to be tough, strong and manly. It was forbidden for little boys to play with little girls and with dolls. Little boys were guided to engage in rough activities such as playing football; little girls were encouraged to play with dolls and was given a playhouse. The image for girls was to be dainty and feminine (i.e. dress-up, put make-up on like Mommy).

Traditions Challenged

Radical changes in family dynamics emerged in America that challenged the status quo in family practices. The youth culture kicked off a rebellion that helped to move one of the most valuable pillars and foundation in America which is the family. The family foundation represented the backbone of America's traditional moral and family values. Unknowingly, their efforts helped to energize and further advanced the cause of women who were trapped behind the walls of tradition. The youth wanted to offer the same educational choices and opportunities to both little boys and little girls. To encourage girls and boys to go to college and pursue careers. It is worth noting the children born to parents of the 1960s until the present are reared in the spirit of "if it feels good do it" and "it's your thang, do what you want to do"? This mindset remains the gateway for liberalism in modern day family life today which is the cause for much of our decline as a nation.

Transition

In the early 1980s, more than 17 million women were in the labor force which was 44% higher than in the 1970s (Fullerton, 1999). Women were confident that they could hold down a job and take care of their children at the same time. The working mom took on the role of being a "supermom" who could juggle work reports and schedules, finish homework assignments for self and the kids, manage sports activities and birthday parties, etc.-- balancing home and work tasks. However, for women gaining their civil liberties and rights did not come without a price.

Male Resistance

Male retaliation against women was fierce as the battle between the sexes began, expanded, and continues today. The majority of husbands was not supportive of their wives decisions to work outside of the home or return to school. Men were not accepting of coming home from a long day of work to find dinner late or not prepared at all. The men were resentful that the home wasn't kept and running smoothly as they were accustomed. The kids were crying and the home atmosphere was filled with the chaos of change. A man's world and way of living was turning upside down. It was all or nothing for men. Angry males opted out of their marriage relationships, and the divorce rate hit America in tidal waves as the bloody battle persisted leaving many homes and families desolate, broken and abandoned in its furious aftermath. The National Center for Juvenile Justice Fact Sheet reported between 1970 and 1996, the number of divorced persons had more than quadrupled, from 4.3 million to 18.3 million. Change had not only come, but change had come with a high cost.

Family Disintegration

As women held their ground, the familiar family
structure they had once known was now leveled. There
was not a remaining solid structure left upon which they
could build. As a major part of the aftermath of divorce,
women found themselves in the midst of having to make
one of the most difficult choices of their lives. Who
would care for their children? Child care was limited
and practically nonexistent, because in the traditional
family structure stay-at-mothers took care of their own
children. Inconsistency in child care by grandparents,
other extended family members, friends and neighbors
became an unwelcomed challenge for the newly
emerging single parent family. Working mothers
struggled and lamented over having to leave their
children behind. Yet the blowing winds and waves of
change and adversity never ceased.

In 1965, day care centers were at a rate of 6% in
America and were mainly used by military families
("Working Mothers"). Women who were once stay- at-
home moms had emerged by joining the majority of
working single moms who were also juggling their new
role as the family's primary breadwinner. The stress of
juggling both male and female roles was a constant
emotional mayhem for working mothers. Also, learning
how to daily cope with the mental and emotional upset
of trying to "fit" in a male dominated workforce caused
additional stress and agitation. Their next greatest

challenge would be how to parent, manage and construct a new family structure from the broken, damaged, and scattered remains of the traditional family, all at the same time. Obviously mothers had to make Difficult Different Decisions (DDD) in learning how to move forward in their new roles outside of the family as well as within the family.

Motherhood

Remaking Motherhood (1987) by Anita Shreve documented the working mother's family struggles as they were unfolding in record numbers during the 1980s. The adverse circumstances and challenges that were surrounding working mothers greatly influenced their on-the-spot spontaneous decisions. Working mothers could not predetermine whether the long range effects of their decisions would produce favorable or unfavorable outcomes for future children and their families. However, working mothers in the 1980s left some open-ended, and unanswered questions for the millennial generation parents. Listed below are the entire twenty-one questions from the book for your review and information. Questions sixteen through twenty-one are the ones to be answered by the millennials. It is the task of working mothers today to continue the work of redefining and remaking the meaning of motherhood.

1. What impact does the presence of a working mother in the home have on children?
2. Does a working mother shape the way a child perceives what mothers and women do in the world?
3. Will daughters of working mothers experience less guilt and conflict for future generations?
4. Will motherhood be perceived as being closer to the current notion of fatherhood?
5. Will children begin to experience their mothers in the same way a previous generation experienced their fathers?
6. Does changing the concept of motherhood affect a child's formation of his or her sex role?
7. Will children come to regard male and female roles as interchangeable?
8. Will the parental role become androgynous?
9. Will sons of fathers who share parenting tasks grow up to be more nurturing themselves?
10. Will nontraditional working mothers encourage a daughter to adopt an achieving, competent, nontraditional role?
11. Will upcoming generations of working women grow up believing that a breadwinner required adopting a male role model or incorporating a female role?
12. Will sexual stereotypes be erased or reinforced?

13. Will children pattern themselves after their mothers and fathers in a way they never had before?
14. If working mothers present their children with more options, will they be able to meet the challenge of having so many choices?
15. Will a child be overwhelmed by having to live up to the standards of two achieving parents?
16. If a mother is largely absent, will it matter to the child if others are able to provide loving and nurturing when she is away?
17. Do the potential benefits of having a working mother present in the home outweigh the consequences of her absence for eight hours a day?
18. Will children growing up in the eighties grow up with fundamentally different notions of mothers, fathers, women, men, self, society, work, home and family than any generation before them?
19. What exactly would these be, and will it make them better persons, parents, bosses and workers than their parents were?
20. Will these changing perceptions create a healthier society?
21. Will the world as the sixties generation knew it be recognizable in thirty years' time, twenty years' time, ten years' time?

I have added a few questions of my own that I see as

challenges for the 21st century mothers as well to consider.

1. How can working mothers prepare their children for unlimited uncensored television, internet, movies, videos, music and games?
2. Why is the millennia noted as the *blame* generation?
3. Define the present parent-child relationship.
4. How can mothers prepare their children to cross language barriers and how to handle racial difficulties?
5. How can mothers prepare their children to handle hidden dangers i.e. drugs and firearms at school, terrorists acts, gangs/violence, peer pressure and bullying?
6. How can mothers prepare their children to drive automobiles and apply good manners?
7. How can mothers prepare their children to care for the environment?
8. Are healthy parent-teacher-child relationships still relevant?
9. Do moms and dads feel good about the family and their roles?

Provided at the beginning of the chapter are definitions of motherhood that deserve the critical attention of 21st century working parents to assist with completing their assignment. By examining these definitions, it can help to determine, identify, and prioritize the questions that would have the most impact in turning around America's present course.

Time To Reflect

In moving forward, womanhood must be acknowledged and recognized as a key ingredient that was missing in the role of women. It must also be recognized for the serious and uncertain risks that were taken by courageous women as a necessary step in reaching their goals of achieving their liberty and freedom. Women must now however, think, rethink, and think again that children are our most valuable natural resource. Children had to compromise, sacrifice, and do without their mothers while they were in the process of discovering and developing their "womanhood". Motherhood today is viewed by some as an interruption to womanhood's ongoing achievements, careers, business pursuits, and interests. The disclaimer by some working mothers "not to parent their children" has caused multifaceted and undesirable social upheaval in America. The cost of freedom left homes broken, and family relationships severed in its aftermath.

It's Motherhood's Turn To Lead

To meet the needs and demands of today requires that motherhood have more flexibility, and to be more inclusive of the expanding potential that has been found in womanhood. Also, the "woman" in womanhood now has to further fulfill her purpose by redefining the true meaning and understanding of her responsibilities and duties that are required of motherhood. To complete the task of redefining motherhood, it must be given first place in leading the recovery efforts to help heal and restore our children. The role of motherhood must become the focus and priority for women. One of the primary roles and responsibilities of motherhood is to parent the children. Motherhood is the anchor that holds the home and family together. Motherhood can no longer be the backseat observer watching the pain caused to her children due to her absence without claiming personal ownership. Motherhood is and remains vital to the sustainability of a thriving humanity. It ranks equally high in the overall structure and composition of the family. New perceptions of the role of stay-at-home Mom's must be discovered.

Children must again become the number one priority of parents. Mothers are the answer to children's needs. Motherhood cannot be perceived as an item to be packaged and outsourced as a commodity. The gift that motherhood carries is the ongoing nurturing of those life sustainable human attributes which is by far of more worth and value, than the acquisition of wealth, achievements, possessions and personal fulfillment could ever offer. Motherhood is equally as important as womanhood and can no longer be compromised or denied its place of full engagement and interaction with her life giving gifts to bring wholeness and well-being to her offspring. The two working together side by side in harmony, and not in competition with the other, helps the making of womanhood and motherhood a total and complete package for humankind. Isn't it time for children sacrifices to end? Isn't it time for them to stop paying the price for women's freedom and liberties, and to start enjoying the benefits and fruits of having both woman-mother too?

Is family life better today? Did the change make our kids better? We must wake up to examine the evidence that is around us in order to answer these critical questions. We must also be willing to take a critical look at the positives and the negatives brought on by these changes in a mother's role. We must assess and prioritize the damages that have been done to children and their family life in the name of progress. I further suggest that working mothers today with children under the age of 18 will use these questions and add new ones to form and begin discussion groups on the critical issues. Organize and hold group meeting in your homes, schools, churches and throughout your communities to collectively determine what is in the best interest of children. The greatest task is for all mothers to join forces and together combine shared experiences and knowledge to extract the best qualities that are indispensable in both womanhood and motherhood. Putting the issues out on the table will end the internal struggle of which is the preferred dominance and focus on achieving wholeness.

Chapter Six

MEN ON THE RUN

The traditional role of males in American families and in society drastically changed as the social movements of the 1960s were emerging. In this dialogue with men there will be many issues and thought provoking questions for males to consider in evaluating their current roles, and to look at how the social events of the past have influenced their life decisions. We will examine the "Big Four Decisions" of the rebellious 1960s on marriage, family, drugs and sex that have taken America off course and put us in what I call the "danger zone".

Bad decisions of the past have gone unchallenged for over four decades that have brought about toxic consequences for us today. Their visible signs and negative outcomes were ignored as they begun to surface. We must ask why they were ignored and why their lengthy existence was allowed that now is responsible for our urgent social crisis. I ask the men that as you journey with me to have an open mind and heart. I also ask you to give your attention to any solutions that you may find along the way that could help restore damaged families in America. More importantly, I ask that you will join in efforts that will help to redirect misguided children who have lost their way.

As men you are important, you have a place, you have a role to play, and you are needed!

Cohabitation

The counterculture sought alternative ways for unmarried couples to live together in order to avoid conformity to traditional marriages like their parents. While cohabitation in the sixties was on the "down low", today it has mushroomed into a trend that is the preferred choice of lifestyle by the majority of Americans. Divorced couples plus unmarried singles living together boosted and set the trend for single parent families in America. This trend was further fueled by a booming sexual revolution that made cohabitation an even more attractive lifestyle. The growth of this trend also was especially attractive to males who opted to flee from the commitment and responsibilities of caring for a family for the chance to have a lifestyle that was unrestrictive. The 2000 U.S. Census Bureau reported the number of cohabitating couples increased tenfold between 1960 and the year 2000 ("Living Together"). The real challenge in this lifestyle are the barriers and oppositions in relationships that it would later present to future generations of singles who would experience difficulty in forming relationships that would end in marriage. Important values that are derived from couples being committed to each other would be removed as well. Commitment helps to aid the maturing process by providing the stimulus for couples growth in becoming their better selves.

This trend's expanded outgrowth was women having multiple children from multiple partners. Fathers are either absent or not actively involved in their children's lives. This expansion strengthened the existing social crisis that was already in progress. Men seemingly impregnated women without the intention of fathering the children. If fathers like J. Williams who was brave enough to come out of his man cave, it would make this negative profile of men disappear. Mr. Williams coming out took place on a major television network as he stood up to openly admit that he was the father of 34 children by 17 different women, and that he wanted to make a change. He is not the only man to secretly live this lifestyle. Many women fell victim to this lifestyle because they wanted men in their lives, and it was the only option they were given. Their willingness or unwillingness to participate was predicated upon their level of their need not to be alone, and empty promises that were not kept.

Passing A Broken Baton

The unwillingness of males to participate in committed relationships is very problematic in today's culture. I admit to young males that since the older generation(s) did not effectively model problem solving skills, they failed in showing you how to resolve conflicts in relationships. It was easier for them to just walk away and let the house and everything in it go up in flames. Their mistakes perhaps is what has caused you to look away from marriage as well, and seek other options for companionship that would cause you less pain and struggle. Many of you are children of divorced parents and have made the choice <u>not</u> to marry based on the terrible childhood experiences that caused you a lot of pain, heartache, and sorrow. You witnessed and felt your parents' rage and anger towards each other and directed some of it at you. You felt helpless as you witnessed your family fall apart. However, making critical life decisions from a place of hurt, disappointment and pain will not heal your pain, or correct the mistakes that your parents made; but will only provide the fuel for it to continue growing. The tidal waves of change that was rapidly occurring in America during the sixties brought out the best as well as the worst in families and society as a whole. Some of you perhaps have never seen a good marriage modeled, but there are couples out there who were able to successfully weather the storms of change and held their families together. The question is for you to decide will you pass the broken legacy to your children.

Real Talk

In an all male discussion group that I once facilitated, I asked the men, Why would they make a conscious choice to have unprotected sex with women who already had several children by multiple partners? And, what hindered them from making the right choice as men to be responsible and use protection? Their answer was both astonishing and unacceptable to me. Unanimously, their answer was because the women "allowed" them to do it. It was the consensus of the group as well to give themselves permission to act irresponsibly, and refuse to be a father. I also asked, Where was their sense of compassion to the women who were obviously weighed down with problems? Having this knowledge, Why would they then choose to repeat the cycle too by walking away leaving their seed behind? The male sentiment, I'm willing to make a baby, but I am unwilling to be a father to one. This male attitude reinforces why fatherlessness has become an epidemic in the American culture. Where was their self-respect and the respect for other lives?

Can you imagine the feelings of children who have never had a daddy, and yet learn they not only have siblings, but siblings from multiple women other than their mother? It is my hope that after reading this chapter, the male consciousness and awareness will be aroused to such a degree that men would become awakened out of their sleep and take immediate action.

Time to Reflect

What has been the ongoing consequences of having unrestrained sex? Has cohabitation made relationships better today? Are we having the results that we want? Have these trends proven to be in the best interest of their children or adults? Who benefits the most? Are we happier and better people? Males must now address long term disregard of the consequences that have followed the 1960s views on marriage and commitment. The 1960s made their decisions based on how they saw marriage , now we must make our own assessment based on our current needs. Families and society are already facing unthinkable consequences with our children as a result of the sixties bad decisions. Today children rule and kill their parents rather than choosing to honor them. Now, we must say it is enough that the majority of young men's story line begin with, "I'm from a broken home"; "I grew up without my father in the home." It is enough for young women's story line to read, "I want to get married, but I cannot find a man that's willing to commit." What hope is there for a better tomorrow for future generations when their parents are not willing to stand up and show them the way by their good example?

Fatherlessness

Fatherlessness is a "first" that we cannot be proud of because it represents one of the many social conditions that have contributed to America's decline as a nation. It is also one of our strongest indicators that America is off course. However, the principal cause of fatherlessness today is by paternal choice. Never before in America have so many children grown up without knowing what it means to have a father. Never before have so many children been voluntarily and intentionally abandoned by their fathers. In 1990, more than 36 percent of all children in our nation lived apart from their fathers— more than double the rate in the 1960s (Popenoe, 1996). Fatherlessness is the leading cause of declining child well-being in our society. " It is the engine driving our most urgent social problems," says David Blankenhorn, author of Fatherless America (1995). What can be done to reverse the trend of fatherlessness? Death and war were the main contributors of fatherlessness in the past. Fatherlessness today is a major derivative of the 1960s sexual revolution. Teenage pregnancies also are among the contributors of this widespread epidemic (like father, like child).

For the first time in our nation's history, millions of men are voluntarily and intentionally abdicating fatherhood. I am not saying that the traditional marriage does not have its flaws. I am suggesting that it can be worked out. By collectively taking on the task to help eliminate the flaws in marriage and include renewed perspectives on what works is perhaps a possible solution that can help to mend our broken families. In the past, fathers and mothers were in committed relationships and governed themselves by higher standards and moral principles that promoted and sustained the quality of life that is rarely seen today. For example, in the past marriages did not infect society with social epidemics such as fatherlessness that is now one of the leading factors that is destroying America from the inside out.

The Cries of the Fatherless

Like never before, the voices of fatherless children in America are crying out that something has gone awry. Their weeping is being openly expressed through their inappropriate behaviors of wanting their fathers to return and be an active part of their lives. Tireless government and community surrogates have made unending attempts trying to fill the void of father absenteeism in the lives of children. These well needed and intentional efforts have painstakingly surrendered to the realization that no other entity can satisfy the deep and longing void in a child's heart like its father. Nothing can silence their cries or fill the missing space in their hearts that is designed only for their father. From the successful older adult male child to the youngest male child, all have cried silent tears, all have openly wept over the pain and hurt that life without their father causes them; so much so that they cannot find escape, peace or rest from its grip. The absent father's status or his condition is irrelevant to the hurting children who constantly wrestle with feelings of rejection and loneliness by being separated from the person who bears their own image and likeness. Children young and old must not be left out on the field of life without their fathers being there to coach them.

Once angered mothers have also conceded that a mother's love alone cannot fill the void that is so deeply embedded within the hearts of their children from missing their fathers. This void surpasses a mother's love. Children instinctively know that their fathers are the missing "peace" because in their hearts they can sense and feel the void on the inside of them. Men argue today that women are not doing a good job in raising the children on her own, yet remain unwilling to step up and activate the responsibility of being a father because you also love your children.

Resource Development

Leading up to the 1960s America was a child driven nation that valued children as one of its most valuable natural resources. Parenting was the biggest and most important job that parents had in America. Parents took the responsibility of their jobs as the primary caregivers and overseers of their children very seriously. It was the job of ensuring that each generation developed the stamina and skills they needed to carry forward to the next generation. They ensured that sound life giving values were sustained by proper nurturing and care. By having active parents who were on their job as parents, America was guaranteed to have educated, law-abiding citizens, safe communities, low health risks, high marriage rates, low divorce rates, and respect for authority figures which made us great as the leading and powerful nation in the world.

Parenting Shift

The counterculture, however, challenged and rebelled against the parental restrictions that were placed on them as children. They created a shift in parenting by rejecting all of the parenting practices of their parents to make room for how they would later parent their children. They wanted to loosen the restrictions and to give their children the freedom of choice and to make their own decisions without parental interference. They desired the flexibility of using a more hands off approach to parenting. They wanted their children to be more liberal and to give creative expressions to life.

Today's method differs from the "old school" basic child rearing practices such as: (1) Parents set and established the boundaries, and taught their children to know where and what their place was within those boundaries; (2) children were given rules by their parents and they were expected to follow them (they did as they were told); and (3) failure to carry out parents instructions resulted in natural and human consequences administered by parents. There was little need for correctional facilities because parents were doing their job.

The shift in parenting has produced over four decades of children who have never been parented by their biological parents. This translates into children who have not been taught sound values and standards of good behavior. Children who lack self-control and their ability to relate properly with others. They also have not been taught how to have and show respect for authority figures, and to express themselves appropriately which are all caused by a deficit in parenting. Parenting practices may have seemed very restrictive in the past, but alongside children behaviors today that are uncontrollable—too much freedom without some restraint is not in their best interest as well.

The lack of properly parenting children is the main source and missing piece that is causing frustration in our schools and communities today. As I stated earlier, the duties and responsibilities of a parent cannot be outsourced in the same mindset that you would drop off your laundry at the dry cleaners and be given a date when they are ready for pick up. Parents drop their children off at day care centers and schools today having that mentality.

Liberal Parenting Practices

The modern family remains a work in progress that is without a clear, definable family structure in place (fathers are missing). Additionally, the composition of modern day families are diverse. A solid family base cannot be established and maintained without all of its missing pieces coming together. Also, the fact that the dynamics of family life are still being transformed makes it very challenging to set and establish common values and practices that are peculiar and suitable to meet everyone's needs.

Families today may not necessarily be governed by rules in the home, and there may be unclear boundaries for children to follow. Parenting practices have unclear and undefined standards for governing and correcting children's behavior. Consequences for wrong behavior is seldom practiced and viewed as a thing to be avoided when possible. However, parents instinctively go into the protective mode, quickly to respond, and to intervene on their children's behalf to prevent and block the threat of real and natural consequences from being administered by other authority figures. Parents oftentimes become defensive and make a quick shift by blaming others of having a lack of sensitivity towards their children. When in fact the action taken by other adults should send parents a message of their need to know the value of consequences and to learn how to use them in correcting and rewarding behavior.

Also, parents should establish and enforce consequences in the home. Teaching consequences will help parents to build their children's understanding and knowledge of their value and purpose as they are growing and learning how to become self-disciplined. Instead parents have opted to defer this task onto the schools, caregivers and the communities. As an unspoken and general rule of modern day parenting, parents either ignore or do not give their children consequences for bad behavior. Children are free to make their own decisions with little or no parental engagement. Promises, money and possessions are used as incentives for correcting inappropriate behavior. "I promise to spend more time with you if__ "; "I will pay you $5.00 for each passing grade"; "I will buy you the latest video game if__."

What is found in the modern family's landscape is that both parents have careers and jobs regardless of their status. Absentee fathers and mothers are responsible for the rearing of their children in a technological home environment that has been proven to harm unsupervised children. Technological driven homes have alienated children from nature, contributed to childhood obesity, and exposed children to sexual predators and traffickers. I ask the question again: Who is raising America's children? The answer is the schools, daycare centers, the media, technology, etc. which cannot do the job of parenting. The job of parenting today must shift from the position of completely hands off or limited childrearing to full-time engagement with hands on childrearing. Parents must reevaluate their priorities by taking back the controls that was handed over to the media, technology, entertainment industries, etc.

Regain Parenthood

Families of today have an awesome opportunity to help turn America's families and children crises from challenges into celebrations. Young mothers and fathers can help America best in this critical hour by teaming up and turning their focus and attention back to the children and family by making the parenting of their children their number one priority. Parents must come together and make a conscious decision to do what is in the best interest of their children. The future of America also demands that children be at the center once again and highly valued with their parents as their most important resource.

Children have made all of America aware of their pain caused by the distractions and abandonment of their parents to other interests. For decades, abandoned children have been acting out to make everyone aware of their pain with little or no lasting results. For their behavior they have been place in perpetual "time out" known as incarceration. Today children are lost and out of control. Unconsciously, parents have taught their children to think and act as adults even though they are children. In response, the courts have said if children commit crimes like adults, under the law they will be treated like adults. Children unrealistically are expected to behave like adults. These are unrealistic expectations that have been placed on children because of overzealous parents to make them independent. Parents also make adult decisions that will impact their children's lives, and yet give little or consideration of how their children might feel about their decisions. An example of this is parents who decide to allow their significant others to move in with them. Parents justify their decision by assuming that children are very resilient and have the capacity to get over things more quickly. Yet repeatedly, children's actions and behavior have proven their assumptions to be wrong.

Children must be seen and treated as human beings first and foremost having the same (yet undeveloped) human tendencies as adults. If it is not easy for adults to cope and manage sudden change, the same holds true for children. Adults are not born from one human species and children born from a different species; both come from the same. Children learn their behavior through observing their parents' and other adults behaviors.

Sexual Revolution

The sexual revolution that emerged in the sixties gave couples the social acceptance and freedom to have premarital and extramarital sex without the fear of unwanted pregnancies. In making a decision of this nature and magnitude, the question before us today is what was the main thought behind this decision? Who would be the chief beneficiaries from this decision? What was to be gained? After all, the original goal of social change was to change America for the good of all. The sexual revolution was a shift in thinking from having sex as a act of procreation, to having sex just for fun and pleasure. The meaning of sex changed from a coercive act to a consensual act. Free love and free sex became the mantra of the counterculture that was highly motivated and promoted. The evolution of sex has added its share as well in a declining America and has produced its fair share of social mishaps.

Prior to this shift in consciousness, couples did not openly show their affection for one another in public places. Being in committed relationships was the acceptable and appropriate channel for having sex. The idea of free love and sex came to mean a lot of different things to a lot of different people for a lot of different reasons. The idea of what was sexually appropriate and inappropriate was dependent upon the viewer's perspective. It was acceptable for men to have sex outside of their marriage as long as they didn't get caught. In this way, the sanctity of marriage was kept intact as well as the ability to have outside sexual relationships. This double standard of conduct did, however, create conflict in the marriage the same as it does in relationships outside of marriage. The same sexual practice for men was not true for women. With the sexual revolution, women now were no longer willing to wait until they were married to have sex either. In fact, public nudity came to be seen as an expression of free love and sex. Couples could be seen making out in public facilities (i.e. parks, concerts, malls etc.).

A Changing Perception

The idea of free sex made it possible for men to have their cake and eat it too, and liberated women to do the same. The idea that a man could no longer enjoy the security and pleasure of being the "only" man in his woman's life was lost, and it created a fury and rage within him. The taking away of "being the only", diminished the specialness that brought him fulfillment in committed relationships. Sexual liberation for women also changed men's perceptions of women, and it was expressed through foul name calling, by referring to women as bitches, and whores which greatly reduced the status and standards that men had previously held for women.

The sexual revolution further gave men and women the freedom to openly have sex with as many partners as they chose, and it was acceptable. Women had gained their equality in the bedroom. Infidelity in marriages by both partners then became an additional strain and a large factor in the disintegration and breakup of the American family. Infidelity still remains an issue for couples regardless of the efforts made to gain sexual freedom. Again, how much has America profited from changes that was intended to make it better? The sexual revolution gave couples the luxury to think only of their immediate self gratification and to momentarily disregard the long term consequences that would follow. With this freedom, sexually transmitted diseases increased along with new and deadly diseases such as the HIV/AIDS virus that surfaced in the early 1980s.

Sex Promoted

The sexual revolution changed the way Americans viewed sex. The message of free love and sex rapidly swept across America through movies, television, magazines, books, artists, musicians and other forms of media that helped to reshape and transform our thinking about sex. Sex became a packaged commodity for sale on the grocery store shelf with the same mind-set as buying a carton of eggs. To take this point a step further, the sexual revolution enabled men to cross boundaries that had once been forbidden and off limits. Extra marital sex was a precursor to the development of the trend for unmarried couples living together.

Sex Out of Control

Sex crossed established limits having no respecter of persons, conditions or situations. Sex impacted work-place policies and practices on sexual misconduct and harassment of employees. Sexual assault crimes against women increased. Nursing homes and the elderly became victims of assault crimes. Schools, churches, communities became landfills with sex victims. With the philosophy of the sixties era being "if it feels good do it," unrestrained sex was on its way to getting out of control. It became prevalent for men and women to turn to innocent children for sex by raping and molesting them. Children were lured into the cars by strangers as they walked home from the bus stop or while playing in the park.

Was sex ever intended to become a crime? Were teachers to have sex and children by their students?" Were children ever to be used for pornography and prostitution? The rate of child molestation committed by fathers, significant others, friends and relatives increased. Young males today use raping women and girls as a part of their initiation for gang membership. All of these have lead to America's number one current (and unthinkable) social issue—human trafficking. Women and innocent children are bought and sold as sex slaves because of the insidious shift in the American consciousness of how sex is viewed and expressed. Sex in America today is over a $13.3 billion dollar a year industry ("Morris, 2014). How did we get here? Have we digressed to this level of human consciousness that we are dehumanizing ourselves? Did the sexual revolution fulfill its original intentions or were there errors made along the way that now must be corrected? Is this matter a serious enough cause for us to *think, rethink and think again* how we perceive sex in American society?

Drugs

Drugs are the last of the Big Four Decisions that radically impacted the American society. Drug usage in the sixties came about as part of an experiment that was being "tested" in a controlled environment by scientists and the government. It was thought that LSD usage would be a medical breakthrough for the treatment of patients with mental illness. However, as the counter-culture experimented, the drug was thought of as a way to open up their minds and lead them to deeper levels of spiritual truth that would help change and better the way of life in America. Drug usage became the grand enabler that made it possible for the creation and development of alternative lifestyles, and is the demon responsible for our declining culture and social disasters.

Drugs forced the development of a subculture that drives human behavior in America that is based on lying, stealing, killing, addiction, and uncommitted relationships. Drugs destroyed individual free will and began to control how Americans would think on any subject. Drug usage is the driving force that has shifted the American consciousness away from the path that was to lead and guide us to the rebuilding of an America that was founded on love, peace, justice, and equality for all. However, drugs became a deceptive force that facilitated America to veer off its intended course. America's strong vision and purpose became gradually distorted and weakened as more and more Americans began to self medicate. Drugs, through their addictive power, influenced Americans to passively accept and ignore obvious signs and consequences that it was having on the American culture. Drugs led the way to the debilitating and costly social issues that are challenging the quality of our lives at this present time. Drugs were a distraction that has diverted Americans attention and focus by causing us to become confused about the priorities of life.

There Is A Way Out

Drug usage has caused Americans to fall asleep at the wheel and created an insurmountable amount of passivity to the critical issues of our day through its numbing effects. Drugs like sex may have begun as a good intention, but now has mushroomed into many uncontrollable and inconceivable social issues in America. The elimination of drugs from the American way of life will mark the beginning of the healing process for its citizens. Citizens will wake up and become alert and active enough to do the work that is necessary to turn our nation around. Also, through the elimination of drugs, America's most problematic social issues will be resolved. To make this change, it will require the same enactment and zeal for change as it did in the 1960s. Remember the power of choice--first a conscious decision was made that change was needed and necessary. The decision was then followed by appropriate actions. It is just that simple. Drugs like sex were transformed into a needed commodity that was sold to the highest bidder. The sale of drugs represent over a $100 billion dollar business enterprise in America that significantly undermines education (Economics"). The portion of the U.S. budget spent on drug rehabilitation programs, clinics and long term imprisonments can be reallocated into creating job opportunities, training, and housing improvements that would calm and dissolve the fierceness of drugs devastating impact.   It can be done.

Manhood v Fatherhood

A man becomes a father when he has his first child. This status is fixed-- once a man becomes a father, he is always a father whether he acknowledges it or not. A father is a man who is the parent of a human being. A father transmits and contributes to the identity, character and competence of his children. Moreover, fatherhood is the key to the emergence of the human family and human civilization. Fatherhood obligates men to their biological offspring. Did fatherhood ever challenge manhood, or has fatherhood been a hit or miss status for men? Womanhood challenged the meaning and definition of motherhood that had wrongly defined her true identity based on the biases of society. Womanhood challenged her spiritual and emotional growth and development which allowed her to fulfill the completeness of her true essence. Did the same spiritual and emotional awakening happen for men as well?   Are men willing to open up and allow their true essence to evolve? Somewhere along the way manhood got stuck in boyhood causing men's development to full maturity to become stagnated.

Boyhood Reigns

Boyhood is a stage of male development that is characterized by self-centeredness, conscious of his looks and appearance, daydreams how fast he can run, how fast he can jump, interest in playing games and athletic events, competition with peers, pride in his masculinity, strong interest in girls and sex. Today, grown men are exhibiting and can be characterized by these same behaviors. Grown men dressing the same as young boys is an example. Failure in men to spiritually mature has hindered their growth and development to successfully enter fatherhood. Fatherhood is stagnant and is waiting for manhood to wake up and to catch up. Manhood has successfully demonstrated man's natural ability to father a child while yet lacking the confidence and certainty about his innate qualities and abilities to be a father and to do what fathers are supposed to do.

A Position Not Covered

Young males are lacking true male role models. They lack a clear understanding of the commitment and obligations that fatherhood and healthy relationships demand. Mothers take their sons to the silver screens and athletic fields for their sons to see and use male actors, athletes, and coaches as their male role models. Sadly, there are no personal male relationships in the child's life to foster and nurture the image that was presented to him on how to be successful. In actuality, most movie stars and sports celebrities are lacking as whole men within themselves too. They share the same pain and anguish as their peers of growing up without a father figure. On the other hand, young males may be clear about their roles and responsibilities as fathers, but by not having a father figure in their lives have made a conscious decision determined not to repeat the pattern left by their fathers.

As a consequence of stagnated fatherhood, generations of males continue to miss this vital benchmark. Multitudes of young males cease to transition into fatherhood while their fathers who want to be boys are spectators and watch as sideline observers. One of the primary responsibilities of a father is to ensure that his legacy is transferred to his son and for ongoing generations that come after him. Generations are being held back and cannot move forward.

Who Carries The Ball?

Mothers cannot teach their sons how to become men. Mothers can teach their sons how to treat women, loyalty, how to develop good character, etc. Mothers in general do not take their sons fishing or show them how to make minor repairs around the house or how to be a father. However, with the proliferated practice of men who are retreating from fulfilling their parental duties and responsibilities as fathers has generated decades of children who are without father. This is a toxic trend and epidemic that must be interrupted and stopped by courageous men. To address this epidemic talk shows and books have been written trying to connect men with women using various methods and strategies.

Men Have Hurts

Not much is said about men and what their needs are. Not much encouragement and attention are given to the plight of men and what can be done to help them to stand up again on their own. Men carry the burden of failure because they have been defined by how much money they have and not by his character. More need to be done overall to help men to build up their self-esteem, self worth, and to remove the negative images reminding them of their failures. Mediation and mental health services are needed to help men find their true identity, and to help heal their mental and emotional wounds of the past. Fathers need understanding. Fathers need assistance with reconciling their relationships, and learning how to become responsible parents to their children. America will need more programs, funding and clinics designated for the sole purpose of reconciling broken families and rebuilding relationships. Such programs as mandatory parenting training, job training, scholarships, mental health and other supportive services that may be needed in helping to rebuild the family. Government spending could be reduced and funds reallocated from funding used for foster care, jails, prisons, wars and welfare to programs that are relevant.

For the sake of young male fathers and fathers-to-be who may not have known why America is facing such unthinkable social crises today, this historical information will help to equip you with the knowledge that you will need to make better informed decisions on these same critical social issues that have carried over into the present. It is my hope that your approach to these critical issues as they have been unfolded may inspire you to become a social activist for change in our present day.

Chapter Seven

DRUGS GONE WILD

The introduction of drugs into mainstream America was one of the Big Four Decisions of the 1960s. Drugs was the lead engine of social change to take America off course and continues to maintain its destructive edge today. Historically, the plan of the Hippie Movement (counterculture) was the promotion and use of drugs as a means of opening up the human mind to achieve deeper spiritual enlightenment. That was a big mistake!

Critics at the time believed America was spiritually stagnated. The hippies wanted their minds opened beyond where they were spiritually. They wanted a means that would affect social change in a way that would lead society to a higher and better way of life. Their plan failed without question. Promoting the use of drugs has led humanity down a long, deep, dark, degrading, and spiraling path of self-destruction. As a society, we know that the untrained mind cannot determine the side effects and reactions that drugs will have on a person. Each individual has his own unique make up and experiences while under the influence of drugs. It is the same for a person's mind and motives; you cannot determine a person's thoughts, intentions, and reactions while they are under the influence of drugs. To illustrate my point, scientists viewed the hallucinogenic LSD as a drug that doctors could use to help heal people with mental illness. The government viewed the usage of LSD differently. During the experiment one of the civilian volunteers liked LSD so well that samples were taken illegally and manufactured for his personal use. Later its widespread usage was promoted to the youth of America. Initially, LSD was freely given away to college students at acid parties that were sponsored off-site. Later, a business empire was built on the sell and distribution of LSD to drug addicted followers. It had become a common belief among users that drugs were the answer to the spiritual dryness that had America stagnated.

Blowing the Winds of Change

Since the beginning of the distribution of drugs into mainstream America, drug usage has persisted with damaging winds that are powerful enough to injure, destroy, and level anything in its pathway. Widespread drug usage can be found throughout society from the highest to the lowest, from the school house to the church house, rich or poor, male or female, boy or girl, educated or uneducated, famous or not famous and young or old. It is all about the money with no value or respect for human lives.

Preparing to Lift Off

Citizens also have become familiar with the quiet, unassuming and undetected waves that drugs carry as they flow deceptively into people's lives to destroy their

character and rob them of their personal integrity.
Drugs in America were once welcomed and received as
an inviting liberating guest and friend that came among
us, and willingly carried us anywhere that we wanted to
go. This friendship would later change the name of the
game by taking away our self-control. Drug usage has
persevered in changing and controlling the way society
think. According to traditional wisdom, Whatever or
whoever controls your mind, controls you. No one is
exempt or isolated from the presence and stronghold
that drugs have on all of society. What matters the
most in drug usage is the reaction and response that
drugs have on the user that can either be positive or
negative. For example, former and present
entertainment artists who have survived drug abuse tell
us that some of their best songs were written while they
were under the influence of drugs. Athletes have
weighed in by their own confessions that they
consistently won sporting events when using drugs.
The long term end result of the residual effects that
drugs have on users supersede the good.

Regenerating the Culture

We know that using drugs is not good by the massive
number of abusers whose lives have been destroyed. We
also know that the addiction controls the abuser which
forces the rest of society to live lifestyles that are fear
based. Living in an addictive society affect our ability to
conduct our daily routines and make sound business

decisions that begin by factoring in the possibility of what could go wrong by employees, coworkers, family members, etc. who are abusing drugs. The need to give the behavior of the abuser consideration causes the rest of us to operate in abnormal behavior. With this deviation decisions are now made from a double minded perspective that society have accepted as our new normal. The abuse of drugs has tarnished society's ability to think correctly. Drugs do possess power that can sway your thinking and they have successfully influenced our society to accept the abnormal behavior and conditions of drug users as normal out of fear of their unknown, bizarre, and sporadic behaviors. The influence of drugs helped to reshape the character of America as well.

Family Intruder

Drug usage whether legal or illegal is the "giant" killer of our day that must be confronted and eliminated. In the olden days, a giant named Goliath was brought down by a brave kid with a rock. We also must believe that it is possible for us to evict, un-invite, and treat drugs as an unwanted guest and killer of our day. Drugs have been allowed to move into our homes and families, our communities, our schools, our government, our businesses, our entertainment, our sports and our daily affairs by taking over and leaving us in despair—a defenseless and hopeless people. Drugs have crept into our homes through addicted family members who began to destroy the foundation of the family's values, morals, trust and honesty through their lying, stealing, cheating, and other destructive behaviors to help feed their addictions. Families were torn apart while society watched as helpless and fearful bystanders.

Before substance abuse education and programs were established, parents were defenseless in fighting off their attackers. Initially, parents were astonished and in disbelief that their children could get involved in drug activities. Drugs as the intruder in the home also blemished and destroyed the family's integrity. Parents were ashamed because they had lost control over their children that went against the expectation of society. Grieving parents sought ways to privately keep the addiction a family secret. Children who were living in the home and were under the control of drugs, openly and boldly rejected the guidance and defied the instructions of their parents. Often out of fear of exposing their children to unknown dangers that could possibly cause them further harm, parents would reluctantly give in to the demands of their drug addicted children. The parent-child relationship was gradually reversed from that of child submission to the parent's authority and leadership, to the parents' submission to their child's reckless and irresponsible behaviors. These ongoing conflicting views and rebellion between parents and children have persisted in homes across America.

Families Taken Hostage

The accepted practice for parents was to send their uncontrollable addicted children to rehabilitation centers to help calm them down when their behavior became too unmanageable for them to handle in the home.   Today, on TV talk shows such as *Dr. Phil,* *Addiction and Intervention,* brave parents have openly admitted to personally funding their children's drug addiction out of fear. Parents were fearful of their children being out on the streets buying drugs, living on the streets, or forced into prostitution, etc. to feed their habits. They opted to pay drug dealers to deliver the drugs to their home.

Additionally, drugs enabled children's capacity to not conform to their parents' lifestyles and beliefs, and to become more rebellious and confrontational. Children who had their own money initially were able to finance their own drugs through their allowances, but as their need and demand for drugs increased, more finances were needed. Children stole money from their parents' wallets and purses. Children stole and sold their personal items as well as household items belonging to their parents to buy drugs. If parents questioned their children about missing items, the children would lie and deny knowing anything about the missing items.

Breakdown of Trust

Parents became more fearful of leaving their children at

home alone because they could not be certain of what they would do if they were left unsupervised. Family trust, one of the main pillars within the family structure has been weakened and/or severed in American homes because of the presence of drugs. Addiction distorts the climate in the home environment, and influences the way families begin to think, see and relate to each other. The normal and natural way of seeing things becomes anesthetized.

Drug Dependency

In homes where parents were already addicted to drugs, the oldest children became their caregivers. Addicted parents were not able to provide for their children's basic needs. Addicted parents would leave home in pursuit of drugs and would be gone for days leaving their children behind without food, water, heat, electricity, clean clothes, etc. These abandoned children may or may not attend school regularly. They would likely become homeless since the addicted parents' first priority is to support their addiction at any cost. The oldest children would be responsible for the care of everybody living in the home. The oldest child would be responsible for doing the shopping, buying groceries, doing the laundry, cooking the meals, doing household chores, helping the younger siblings with their homework, giving them baths and putting them to bed. Additionally, the oldest child is burdened by the parents' constant theft, coupled with their misuse of family funds.

Addicted parents frequently sold and exchanged their belongings and food to purchase drugs. Children with addicted parents were never in attendance at school events and achievement programs as their peers. Parental addictions forced children to prematurely think and act like adults.

Neighborhoods Taken Hostage

The influx of drugs into the American way of life also swiftly took control of and transformed our neighborhoods and communities into drug and gang turfs where crime and violence reigned. Communities were terrorized, and residents became fearful of the drug and gang lords' threats of retaliation if they showed any resistance to their drug activities. Their presence was so prevalent in the community to the degree that residents lost hope of running them out and learned to live with them. Residents and their children adjusted to hearing and seeing open gun fire, people killed, fighting, selling, buying, and openly using drugs. Drug casualties filled the landscape with crime and violence that held communities under siege. People lived barricaded in their homes and apartments; children were not allowed outside to play; and people were fearful of walking the streets alone at night. Driven by their addictions, drug abusers committed petty thefts within the community and aimlessly roamed the neighborhood streets seeking food, money and other handouts. The sell, distribution and addiction to drugs are the leading forces of

142

degradation and self-destruction of humankind.

Schools Taken Hostage

The energy of drugs continued down its path and made its way into our schools, and have played a major role in their transformation from institutions centered on education and learning into institutions of crime and violence. Items are stolen and resold by students to make expensive purchases and for money to buy drugs. Selling and using drugs permeated school campuses through gang presence and activities. Community drug dealers recruited and convinced the youth that profits made from selling drugs were higher, the money was faster, and success was guaranteed if they joined forces with them. Many youth bought into the idea that deferred gratification was not the path for them to take, and getting an education for them became secondary and/or obsolete. Youth who were recruited blended in with the regular students and attended school every day with no intention of getting an education. With their infiltration into the schools, student handbooks were upgraded to include state law violations that mandate the arrest of students committing violent acts, carrying a weapon, buying and/or selling controlled substances while on school property.

The shift from education to selling drugs for income is indicative of a mind change in a direction that does not promote the best interest of others. The outcome of

143

selling drugs weighs down society with unnecessary threats of the loss of life, property and possessions, broken relationships, and loss of trust. The deception for the youth in making such unwise choices is the realization that selling drugs comes with a price. Their lives become exposed to hidden dangers, and to those around family members this is a high price to pay. The corruption of their character is yet another high cost. This lifestyle is not for the better, but it brings out the worse by forcing youth to become dangerous, and to commit harmful acts to others in order to successfully do their job and to make a profit. To make money that justifies wrong behavior that impedes and distracts from the quality of life for others is unprofitable income.

One of the residual side effects that drugs have made on the youth is the mind-set and belief that they are not good enough. Their belief in themselves is tainted by feelings that they are inadequate within themselves to naturally achieve the things they desire in life. The false belief that reliance on drugs will help them to achieve their life's goals does not reflect sound thinking.

The youth seek drugs that will enhance their performance, help them to lose weight, gain weight, change their looks, build them up, keep them awake, and put them to sleep without any requirement, effort or discipline on their part. They have the attitude that says "a pill is the answer to all of my inadequacies" until the sad day when their dependency on drugs shows up. The misuse of drugs has helped our youth to build and foster a wrong perception of themselves and their abilities that has become debilitating.

Masked Deception

To the religious mind, drugs are descriptive and synonymous with the religious character known as Satan or Devil. Satan is believed to be a fallen angel with followers out to deceive mankind. He is beautiful and loves beautiful things. He is talented and gifted in music and singing. He and his followers ultimate purpose in the earth is to kill, steal and destroy mankind. The Devil also is taught to be a master of deception and the father of all lies. Drugs' impact and influence on society shares the same resemblance, attributes, and characteristics of this religious character. Drug usage creates a euphoria in the mind of the user that causes the loss of self-control while under its influence. Like the Devil, drug dependency denies the truth and operates best by deception. Drug dependency has produced a subculture in America of selfishness, lies, killing, stealing, destroying, excessive pride, human trafficking, poverty, poor health, poor education, and no regard for authority, etc. Victims of drug abuse lose their ability to live by moral principles due to their uncontrollable craving for drugs. Drug dependency incapacitates sound reasoning, grounds and keeps its victims operating in the lower levels of the ego.

Changing Values

The infiltration of drugs into mainstream America made the transition easier for America's image and values to change "for the people" to materialism and greed. Songs and movies were written that deified and created new images that were symbolic of greed and materialism. The love of money became a god to both users and sellers of drugs. Possessions and getting a fix by any means necessary became the creed for living. Making money and ownership are now the lifestyles of choice that are used to promote self grandiosity and extravagance. Satan, the religious figure, has to keep up his image, so vanity is now over a billion dollar industry. In the name of progress, success is achieved by defrauding and deceiving others which contributes to America having the highest incarceration rate in the world.

Confession

Religion was thought to be stagnated by many in the 1960s, I concur. As a child I went to Sunday school every week, attended Vacation Bible School every summer and attended weekly worship services. I faithfully participated in all youth services and all other church sponsored activities. In our church, Sunday school classes went all the way up to older adults. As I drew closer to the older adult class, I was not drawn to the religious tradition that was before me. I would

146

constantly ask myself as I got older, if what I was being offered all there was to look forward to.

Church leaders allowed me to remain in the class for young adults beyond the allotted time until I relocated to another city. I was blind because I could not see a match between the Bible lessons that I was taught and the visible outcomes in the lives of the people that I would later become. Like the hippies, I did not want that type of lifestyle for myself or for my children. I too felt that life had more to offer. Faithful church attendance just wasn't enough for me. There was something missing in my life and I wanted more. I did not however, resort to drugs to help me find the answer. I searched deeper into the teachings of Christianity to help me get to know God more. In my search for deeper spiritual knowledge and fulfillment, I opened myself to all Christian denominations in my search for God. I did not find God in the church building. I experienced God in my heart when I was alone and sitting on my living room floor crying out for answers caused by circumstances that were out of control.

At that time I had physically left the building in my search for God and I refused to return until I had something more concrete to base my life on as well as the lives of my children. In my heart, I knew that I could not teach my innocent children what I did not know to be true for myself. Alone and in pain, I cried out asking God if He was real. I needed to know if the stories that I had been taught in church about Him since my childhood were really true. I also wanted to know if He expected me to conform to the behavior and practices that were found in the building when I was there previously. I wanted to know would I be killed on the spot or be punished by Him if I made a mistake as I had been taught. Surprisingly, I learned that God was not in church dogma and rituals, and allowed me to evolve spiritually on my own and to be myself. I even made mistakes along the way and I'm still alive. After I discovered the presence of God for myself, I later returned to the building and discovered by trial and error how to apply some of the disciplines and teachings to my daily life and decisions that helped in my spiritual development. There were still many errors in the religious teachings of the church that remained ineffective. No matter how I applied my faith, the steps I was taught did not work for me. I also applied my faith to interdenominational teachings and I painfully discovered what teachings worked and the ones that did not work. Many of the religious concepts caused me and my family much difficulty, heartache and disappointments. Not only did I not get the results that I expected, but it caused me to be mad at God for not keeping His word as I had been told. I now know the difference in human ideas about God and God inspired ideas, and there is a difference. My questions about God have been answered because of my personal experience and I am now a seeker of truth.

Renewed Hope

As a nation, we too must come to know truth by
acknowledging that religion as we knew it failed in its
mission to bring people true enlightenment necessary
for them to progress, to live prosperous, and productive
lives. But the failure of religious institutions does not
mean that a Higher Power does not exist or that it is not
real. Nor does it give justification to the decision that
Americans made in the past to use drugs as a medium
for gaining spiritual enlightenment. Both drugs and
religion are representatives of human failures that must
be challenged, corrected, and celebrated. They both are
costly errors that now threaten our future existence as
human beings. Perhaps this finding could be the advent
of both the religious and spiritual communities coming
together in unity to bring the reality of **LOVE** to bear
on an endangered and suffering humanity.

Ready To Recover

The experimentation of drugs in the 1960s may have
been initiated from a place of goodwill and well being,
but it was an experiment that went bad. Are we now
wise enough to recognize the high cost that has been
paid to allow and maintain the unnecessary presence of
drugs in our midst that is causing America to decay
from the inside out? Through bad choices that threw
America off course and changed its direction.
Government spending to fund and operate drug

rehabilitation programs, mental health services, and to building more prisons would be significantly reduced if drug usage was truly challenged. Everyone would become the beneficiaries of an American way of life where government spending could be put to better use in programs (i.e. health care, research, education, job training and higher wages) rather than spending billions to sober up its citizens. Americans cannot consider drugs as a basic necessity in our lives and place it on the same level and category as food, air, water and shelter. All attempts that are made in building new schools, moving into new and higher income neighborhoods, changing cities and states are futile efforts in trying to narrow the chances of escaping the monster that is running wild in our streets. All of these combined efforts will not make it go away. We cannot outrun this unwanted guest that we have welcomed and invited into our homes, schools and communities. Our bad choices must be challenged. Bad choices that are not corrected will repetitively produce negative consequences until the correct decisions are made. We must arise from our stupor and look to our highest inner selves and choose the right path that leads to health, happiness and wholeness.

Chapter Eight

MEDIA GONE WILD

Media overexposure has become a public health threat in America. It is the main cause of childhood obesity. The media has taken us beyond the limits of normalcy in our everyday lives. Ordinary daily life occurrences and events are embellished with half truths and presented to viewers as possible threats of potential harm and danger by making them to appear more or less dangerous than they actually are. Overexposure of the media in reporting the failures and shortcomings of others have ruined the personal integrity of others, destroyed business character, ended marriages, destroyed careers and has left many lives permanently damaged and destroyed. To the undeveloped mind of an innocent child, media overexposure can create an unrealistic and unnecessary fear of the environment. Higher ratings and fear tactics drives the media to bring excessive and continuous daily broadcasting of tragic news stories that feeds the general public. Privacy in America has become a lost form. When is enough, enough? News investigators are constantly looking for anything that can give them a story to report? Where is the end of the media's insatiable appetite for more?

Does it end when media over exposure threaten our well-being and the freedom of the American people no longer exist? Freedom of the press has overextended

151

itself when media exposure of the lives of ordinary citizens have the same plight as the movie stars, athletes, top business leaders and other public figures by the constant invasion of their privacy. The media spotlight shines bright on ordinary citizens when tragedy occurs. News stations pride themselves in being the first at the scene, and getting the exclusive interview showing little or no remorse for the victims and families. This is a classic example of the behavior that America's children see modeled by adults. However, adults have characterized children today as having or showing no remorse. Parents are not the only adults that helps to shape the lives of children. Ordinary citizens and public figures alike cannot privately grieve or mourn their losses without the fear of media exposure and often without their consent. Everybody in America does not need to attend the funeral service of victims of tragedy that is covered by the media. Human error and failures are subjected to ongoing public scrutiny and embarrassment because the media have gathered at their doors, checked into their personal history and backgrounds, etc.

No one is safe and out of harm's way from the media. This behavior has created many phobias in the minds of people as well. Must our homes be inundated by every television and cable station reporting the same tragic events of the day? Why can't news events be shared among them? Must all regular programming be interrupted also? Must Americans be stalked by the press to get a story? America has created this news frenzy, and we can also limit and restrict its usage. Human error need not be exploited for any reason to be viewed as newsworthy.

In the 1960s the media had limits and a cut- off time that was regulated by the federal government. Television and radio stations ended their daily broadcasting at a set time. There was no all night television and listening to the radio. Cable and the internet did not exist. Citizens read the newspaper. By word- of- mouth community events and tragedies were shared. Church members and school officials visited the homes of their students and parishioners to stay connected, informed and to show their support of each other. Together school and church officials also used bulletins and made weekly announcements to notify and share information with their students, and parishioners. Noteworthy news events were also posted throughout the community. The eyes, ears and minds of the people had opportunity to rest and develop other interests.

Though the advancement of technology has significantly advanced our ability to communicate more effectively and more timely; with this advancement a high cost is being paid. In 1975, Walter Cronkite reported on the air that by the year 2000 with the help of technology, the American work week would be reduced to 30 hours giving Americans 10 hours more of leisure time to enjoy the things they had purchased to help make families happy. The advertising industry undermined this prediction by creating images and slogans that told us being busy was the thing to do in order to constantly sell more electronics that continuously change to keep Americans chained to consumerism. Because we now live in a tabloid (star struck-reality shows) society, Americans take sport in delighting and feasting off the weaknesses, failures, hardships and misfortunes of others. To be successful today means that you will be hunted down like an animal by hungry photographers looking to make a kill. When materialism, success and wealth become more valuable than human lives, there are sure to be undesirable consequences.

During a vulnerable period in our history when the institution of the American family was experiencing great turbulence, desperate families turned to television and technology for support with their children. It was a big mistake that was made by families. Single parents used whatever means that was available to them to maintain their jobs and to stabilize their new roles. The television was a trusted and reliable resource that parents had grown up with when they were children. Parents believed it would keep their children safe and preoccupied while waiting for them to get home from work. Parents knew and understood that children would explore and get into trouble when left on their own without adult supervision. They took the risk anyway. Television advertisers seized upon this opportunity to profit, and took control of the desires and minds and imaginations of the children by offering them more and more games, toys, clothing, fast foods, and other forms of electronic entertainment to persuade their parents to buy. It would be a grave error for the creators of technology to disclaim damage and harm it has helped to create through paid advertisement that has helped to shape the behavior of children. Advertisers knew that children were home alone unsupervised, and their parents were looking for creative entertainment that would keep their children busy for hours. Every household was happy, parents believed they had found the solution to their childcare needs, and the children were joyfully being entertained as well. Things couldn't be better.

In this state of euphoria, after the hippie movement was dissolved, the 1960s era utilized the media to carry over into the 1970s the promotion of its ideologies into mainstream America. Television producers began to target the children and their families by creating shows like The Simpsons. Bart and his family became the new role model for American families by making their dysfunctional lives appear humorous and normal. Bart who was very disrespectful to his parents, siblings, neighbors, teachers, the police and all other authority figures became the new role model for children. The

Simpsons modeled what the new American family would look like for children if parenting was less restrictive, and children were allowed to be more creative in expressing themselves. Children in real life began to imitate and incorporated this character in their own lives. Their parents were too exhausted at the end of the day, and trying to adjust to a new way of life to teach their children how to properly handle their pinned up emotions. To hurting children they were able to identify with the character Bart who looked like he was having a lot of fun exhibiting inappropriate behaviors. Remember, children learn by observation and by hearing. The mind of a child is like a sponge, it will soak up whatever it is exposed to because it is unable to discriminate television from real life.

During that season of broken family life, television took advantage of children and their families' vulnerability. If parents were not available to help their children with managing the tumultuous changes in their lives, television through the images of the character Bart and his family, seeds of rebellion were being planted in young minds when families were at their weakest. America would later reap the harvest. Children believed that Bart modeled the proper way for them to express themselves. There was no stopping them. From a teacher's perspective, it is very difficult for students to unlearn what they have been wrongly taught, and to teach a student the correct way. One philosophy in early childhood education states "parents are the child's first teachers." In this train of thought, the media became the surrogate parent and became the child's first teacher (film makers, television, cable, internet, magazines, technology, entertainment, etc.) of America's children.

Movie makers and television producers produced shows that taught young girls how to give up their virginity, and that it was taboo not to have sex. They taught children how to defy their parents authority by breaking their rules in order to do what they wanted (i.e. dating an older boy or man, attending under age wild parties with drugs and alcohol, sneaking boys and girls into the house without their parents' permission, etc.) . Innocent children had their first kiss and spoke their first curse word while on the set of a movie or television show because that was how the script was written. Children were cast in adult roles as well. Also, specific and graphic movie and television scenes showed parents being killed by their children. Many of these scenes and stories were taken from real life tragedies and were embellished by writers. Nothing in society was kept sacred from children, they were exposed to every imaginable and unimaginable circumstance that life could offer. Every value and standard that once governed society have been challenged by movie makers that have helped to steer America off course.

The entertainment industry is filled with sex, crime,

fear, terror and violence. Murderers are given movie and book deals for their heinous crimes and violent acts against others. It is the conduit that keeps America's landscape flowing and filled with negative images, sights, and sounds that are continual contributors that challenges our abilities to maintain peaceful attitudes and minds for achieving a better world that is not filled with such chaos. To achieve stardom, our youth copycat movie scenes by leaving notes behind for filmmakers to follow after they are dead. They want the attention of the world and are willing to gain it by their death if that is what it takes, because that is their perception of how the story has to end. When imaginative and creative advertisers and the entertainment industries collectively visualized and brought fantasy characters to real life, in the minds of children this transformation was real. Abandoned children without adult supervision could not tell the difference between the make believe fictional characters and real life. Nobody told them the characters do not die for real and at the end of the day, they go home and get paid for doing their job well, the same as their parents. Parents as well took their children to malls, shows, etc. for exposure to these fictional characters as their role models without the benefit of having laid a solid foundation of sound moral values and reality within them. The desire to be more, to achieve more became the drive of the parents for their children by characterizing the ordinary life and occupations of the citizens as a dull and boring life.

Media coverage should be censored now to allow children and future generations to grow up in a loving healthy home and social environment. Society should not live in fear of the media but should embrace the good that it has to offer as well. The media should do more to help create a flexible environment where celebrities and public figures can share the same freedom and liberties in the same way as everyone else. Also, the media should help to create an environment where the privacy of everyone is respected. The media can also minimize its power to influence children by not promoting the creation and build up of false images of human beings that makes it difficult and unrealistic for children to live up to and maintain. More celebrities should also be featured as ordinary human beings living ordinary lives. It would help America's recovery efforts by minimizing reporting events that destroy the character of stars who children once saw as their heroes and believed in them. The making and breaking of stars' reputations and character for public view by the entertainment industry should be eliminated. Children don't know the difference, they interpret seeing the shortcomings of their favorite stars to mean that nobody can be trusted and they see the world in that light. The media must share the responsibility to help America to restore and rebuild itself by providing balanced news coverage that is inclusive, fair and promotes the well-being of others.

Advertisers, programmers, sex offenders, drug dealers and criminals all knew that children were alone and without parental supervision. Everyone preyed on this untapped market and it was all about profit. While the children's parents were preoccupied with getting free, gaining wealth, starting businesses and careers—the seeds for the exploitation of children were being sown and nurtured.

Parents could not be in two places at the same time. Somebody had to pay the price because the frenzy was the fear of being left behind and being ordinary. The children are our biggest losers in America. We can play cat and mouse games all we want, but we have to come out of our hiding places of blame and face the realities we have created, and begin to think and do things differently. We have experimented long enough wondering what it would look like if children were not a priority. The results are all in and lie openly for all to see in our documented public and private records. Were we mature enough as a country to handle unlimited media? Have we been able to successfully manage it? The thinkers of our day say it is good to fail because it teaches you from experience what you need to do in order to become successful. This being said where do we go from here to correct the mistake and move forward? We must act responsibly over the media's progress and begin again to manage the media properly and fairly. We must identify the lessons learned and work tirelessly not to repeat the mistakes.

When America shifted from the traditional family lifestyle to conform to false philosophies and fantasy images of celebrities, it opened our focus on external values and images rather than the quest and development of our internal value system.

Chapter Nine

GROUNDS FOR RECONCILIATION

There were a whole lot of shaking going on in America during the 1960s. Social institutions were tested and shaken to their core by the social movements. The people in America had grown restless with the environment and took action. The institution of marriage that houses "the family" is one of the most essential pillars in America that was shaken as well. The launching of the sexual revolution, high divorce rates and the popularity of cohabitation all questioned the core values of the traditional marriage that ultimately led to the disintegration of the family. Fragmented broken families fill America's landscape today. Marriage is associated with pain and something that is to be avoided. There are generations of single parents who remain intimidated and fearful of commitment caused by the heartache and pain they experienced as the by-product of broken homes. These are they who are living out their lives in fear of failure and choose to remain disconnected rather than commit themselves to a relationship. Meanwhile, the lives of children who are the hope of our future lie weighing in the balance.

Efforts to help America change its present course, the need for broken relationships to heal, and the need to offer hope to future generations lay are sufficient in laying the groundwork for challenging and reconciling our personal beliefs and ideologies concerning the institution of marriage and family going forward. To begin the process of recovery, we start by examining the principles of the traditional marriage, gender roles, and the responsibilities of individual family members. Flaws that were hidden in the marriage and family surfaced as life in America had significantly begun to change in the 1970s and 1980s by the pressures of social change. The flaws were hidden in the principles that governed marriage and the family. It became evident that these principles were not inclusive of everyone and did not adequately address the needs of an evolving culture.

Let's examine the ideology that it is by divine will for men to rule women that is taught by traditional marriage. This is the basis for how the establishment of the caste system of male dominance was formed to govern his relationships. The system was implemented through traditional practices that was also set- up for men to rule the women and family. Males were given the advantage in every aspect of the American life which included their business, personal, and family relationships. However, the system could not work effectively without women being oppressed, pressured to surrender and submit their "free-will" unconditionally to be ruled by men. Punishment was instituted for women for failure to comply. "Was this a fair and impartial system?" "Did it offer justice and equality for everyone?" To challenge your thinking on this ideology consider, "What if the establishment of the male caste system was based on a false set of principles and beliefs?" "What if these religious teachings and practices that you have believed and followed all of your life, based your thoughts and the affairs of your life were wrong? What if biblical scholars made errors in their interpretations of the scriptures. (TRTA)?"

Let's consider the justification that was used for this train of thought. According to the creation story in the Bible, the origin of the male and female relationship was interpreted for the man to rule over the woman. It was a logical assumption because the woman was the one who disobeyed God, and also the one responsible for getting her man in trouble with God. Based on this interpretation, man had the right and was entitled to rule over the woman forever by default. Also, the man was superior because he was the "first" one to be created. Women were seen to be weak and was disqualified to be on their own, they needed a keeper. This interpretation helped to form and shape the identity and attitude of the man in who and what he believed about himself and his relationships.

The big question we should ask, "If it is according to divine will that men are to rule in this manner, it also raises the question about the character of God. Is God stern and unforgiving when His followers are taught to forgive others?" Is punishment automatic every time a person makes a mistake? Was the sentence given to women to spend their lifetime in subservience and inferior treatment a justifiable punishment ? Was the erection of barriers that limited and prohibited women's interaction, involvement and participation in society justifiable?

Today, there are men who are trapped by these religious teachings and are unable to move on. Others are waiting behind these religious walls and they strongly believe it is by divine will for them to rule women and they are waiting for God to prove them to be right.

Another male perspective is that some men see themselves as victims of the Women's Rights Movement who are also waiting for divine adjudication on their behalf. These examples are all belief systems in the mind that must be challenged before positive efforts in reconciling relationships can be effective.

I mentioned previously that America's landscape is filled with broken relationships from the past and present that should be our primary focus and, will also deserve our close attention in recovery efforts. Therefore, we must be creative in our approach and initiate efforts that will help to heal, reconcile differences and bridge the gap. The disintegration of the family is all around, and children lives are being destroyed daily; needed men are waiting on the sidelines to be declared the victims; and fighting for the present social order to be reversed.

The big question is "If it is according to divine will that men are to rule in this manner, it also raises the question about the character of God. Is God stern and unforgiving when His followers are taught to forgive others?" Is punishment automatic every time a person makes a mistake? Was the sentence for women to spend a lifetime of inferior treatment and subservient to their spouses justifiable punishment?" Was the erection of barriers that limited and prohibited women's interaction, involvement and participation in society justifiable?

If male dominance and superiority are according to divine will, from this perspective God is seen as an oppressive male ruler who is out to punish when He is not obeyed. Does this ideology reflect a fair and just God who would only punish the women, and reward the men when they missed the mark too? "Was it reasonable for a system based on principles of inequality to women continue to exist? Should a woman be seen and treated as a whole person? Should this misperception of women go unchallenged?"

If the male caste system met with divine approval, was it also divine will for men to abuse women?" On the other hand, if this concept of the true nature and character of the Divine is accurate to be a punisher who is biased against women; we too must consider the lifetime punishment of men that has not yet manifested. With this ideology males cannot go unpunished for their part in missing the mark, for that would make the Divine a

166

respecter of persons. Since the rule of males is the basis for this ideology, it would be the right thing to do to judge males according to the same standards that he has set for others. Since the system places no one else outside of himself to be in charge, then it is the male alone who is solely responsible for our present social crisis and chaotic living conditions. The males are accountable for failure to exercise his authority adequately to govern his family. He is accountable for how he mishandled the break-up that allowed the disintegration of his family. How he has abandoned his wives and children and allowed his home to go up in flames. Under Divine oppression men would be required to give a full account for how they have not restrained their life's flow in causing unwanted children to be born and by failing to stick around to love, provide, and care for them. Men only are accountable for the creation of numerous surrogate childcare and other family support entities due to their failures as ruler. Men would be held directly responsible for their refusal to parent their children; and for allowing them to terrorize communities, threaten authority figures, and to commit deadly acts of crime and violence. Men would be the ones responsible for leaving their children unprotected and susceptible to sexual predators, gangs, hunger, poor health, and incarceration. Ultimately, males are solely responsible for how they have abused their power to rule. Under this ideology, there is no way for males to escape their punishment from an oppressive God.

Did a loving God create humankind solely to punish us if we messed up? As rulers are men willing to face an unmerciful God who is waiting to get revenge at any time? Will men continue to operate in the same mindset that has led us to our present outcomes, or will men take responsibility by correcting and changing their beliefs about the superiority of men?

If religion was not in error "Why would an oppressive God have allowed women to gain their rights and freedom?" This is an opportunity for men to *think, rethink, and think again* their concept of God as a starting point to gaining the knowledge of the truth of God, rather than following the religious traditions of men. In a sense, women's rights was a good thing because it helped to enlighten men about their rights as well. It freed men to establish their true identities, learn their new roles, and to discover new positions within the family and society. The removal of the full burden of responsibility for the total family was liberating because men now have comparable helpers. Men as well gained the freedom to spend more time with their families, and to be father to their children, rather than working long hours and extra jobs to provide for them.

The Season for Change

The family is a basic structure upon which America was founded. If the home is one of the main building blocks and if it is not grounded properly, what hope do we have in trying to put America back on track. Establishing and building harmonious relationships is the birthplace of the family. If couples continue the trend to begin their lives together by establishing their families on a foundation that is lacking in commitment, then the results will be offspring who will carry their DNA to the rest of the world. This is how America operates, the family is the building block that supplies the human resources. If the human resources are flawed, damaged and broken, what is the quality of the products that are being produced? We see evidence of this expanded consciousness throughout America in our politics, businesses, social institutions, etc. where companies and organizations that should be working together are divided and territorial.

The popular trend of couples living together without commitment is a threat to the family that must be challenged and turned into a celebration. Consider how relationships will change for the better as more and more of the stubborn old belief systems of the past were broken down and replaced with renewed and livable ideologies. The need for old unhealed injuries and wounds of the past that has caused couples to fear each other would be acknowledged and help would be provided. Rather than couples resisting, instead they would welcome new changes and would be encouraged to develop strategies that would help to bring unity and healing to America's children and families.

The possibility of reclaiming our personal and family relationships can be achieved by our willingness to make changes in our behavior, the way we think and feel, and to confront what we do not know and believe. Couples who are armed with new perceptions, their relationships would be open to move beyond the current level of stagnation and limitations to explore new possibilities with courage and renewed vigor. New relationships would be truth based and grounded in universal principles and values that everyone could share in beliefs common to all. Also, everyone would be free to be themselves without having to build walls, to create systems that fosters cooperation, interdependence, embraces and accepts individual differences with love, harmony, and mutual respect for each another. The home is the distribution center where the instillation of human values are nurtured and performed. Couples also can change and renew their commitment not to remain separate and equal, but to remain equal and together (TRTA). Remember problems cannot change with the same mindset that created them.

Chapter Ten

THE UNFINISHED COURSE

We know that America is presently off course and yet there is a great opportunity to correct, adjust, and complete the unfinished work that started the social movements in the 1960s. Through proper realignment and significant adjustments in the landscape America will be able to reaffirm its vision and commitment of being a nation where liberty and justice for all can be realized. Although the present social realities to living the American Dream for all may seem overwhelming and impossible for some, by meeting our challenges with a new vision for ourselves makes the turnaround achievable. America's greatest challenges today can also be its greatest opportunities. There still remains hope of recovering from the devastation of our social ills. We not only can reclaim, but we can also rebuild a better America founded upon universal principles and immutable values that will not only strengthen us at the present, but will provide long lasting security for future generations as well.

Social Abnormalities

America is the birth parent of four major social movements that occurred simultaneously in the 1960s.

Much of the social upheaval that America is experiencing are the results of serious afterbirth complications from these movements. To increase our understanding of the social mayhem of today, there are key and essential steps that immediately follows the delivery of a baby. This process includes close observations of the mother and infant by the attending nurses and physicians, a thorough examination of both infant and mother, separation of mother and infant, a detachment of the placenta and clean-up of the delivery area.

The examination following the birth determines the presence of damage or other concerns, the need for repairs, medications or follow-up treatment that may be needed. The examination further ensures that the afterbirth has successfully detached itself from the mother, and it is thoroughly examined. The last step is the clean-up of the delivery area that appears to be very chaotic and out of order but in fact it is not. It is all a vital part of the labor and delivery process. If a step is omitted, the potential for future complications to both the mother and the child is high; and if left untreated, it can be potentially life threatening.

As mentioned earlier, religion in the 1960s in America was stagnated, the country had not matured enough spiritually and emotionally to adequately handle birthing the multiple agents of social change that was occurring at the same time. These social movements spontaneously induced America's untimely labor pains that could not be slowed down or stopped. Change alone is a very difficult process to manage; but when it is forced, change can be met with extremism and harsh resistance. Inevitably when in the midst of change, there will be misunderstandings, hurts, disagreements, mishaps and oversights because the experiences of change does not affect everyone in the same way. However, on a positive note, the stirrings of social change helped America to detach from its old established and rigorous caste system that was hindering its growth and maturity as a leading nation. America's vision was plainly written, but the various paths that have been taken to get there have no doubt created some serious flaws that necessitated an interruption in how it was operating.

America missed some required and vital steps in the afterbirth process of the social movements that followed their delivery. Complete and thorough examinations of each movement individually were omitted that would have detected the presence of damage and would have determined if repairs were needed. Also, an examination would have determined if each movement had successfully detached from the mother appropriately. Consistent routine follow-up check-ups were not provided. Routine examinations occurred as needed, and were based on whose cry was the loudest. Excruciating pain is a warning symptom that signals the possibility of serious injury, infection, or damage. Tragically for America, there was damage that occurred that now had serious complications. The damage has gone undetected and untreated for decades.

Unanticipated Sibling Rivalry

Sibling rivalry was a major barrier of distraction for America as a young parent. America had not been prepared to properly parent the movements she had birthed, meet their growing needs, and the needs of her remaining children. Nurseries for the new babies had not be set-up, and adjustments in the home was needed. As the new babies arrived, the unprepared older siblings refused to make adjustments, and to share with their young siblings. The older children grew very disgruntled with having to share what they claimed were their rights exclusively. Also, the older children had already settled into a way of life that was familiar and predictable in comfortable surroundings. Soon America was in the midst of a long term vicious sibling rivalry that was beyond her level of maturity to control and manage. America was too inexperienced to handle the task of parenting multiple children; unable to neither give them individual attention, nor to provide what they wanted. Out of mounting frustration and to relieve the stress and pressures of parenthood, America agreed to allow her youngest children to have a party. However, the party lasted for an entire decade (1980s). America and her youngest children were having big fun partying, shopping, etc. and enjoying themselves. The President spent the largest amount of money on inaugural activities than any president in U.S. history.   Also during this period, America began exhibiting unexpected wild and reckless behaviors for a parent to do.

America's oldest children did not join the party but instead grew more and more disenchanted with the changes that were occurring. They began demanding America to turn things around and go back to the their old and familiar way of life before she when off and got herself pregnant again. They blamed America for bringing home those unwanted children, and needing their help in taking care of them. This uncooperative attitude permeated and filled the American landscape with guilt, shame, and blame. Disagreements among family members are the natural order of things, and as things change, everyone is not going to agree.

Moreover, America being a youngster herself was easily enticed and consumed by the youthful energies of her youngest children. This also is indicative of a season in American life when parents lost interest in being parents to their children. Instead, parents wanted to be friends with their children because they wanted to get busy getting their party on as well. America went ahead and bought into the philosophy "if it feels good do it." Having this new mantra, the young generation and the old generation lost all forms of self-restraint and the sense of decency. Parents crossed over former barriers that were held by parents to enjoy their new freedom and privilege of partying and drinking with their children. The sensual appetites for a majority of Americans consumed and took total control of their thoughts and behaviors. Sensual pleasures were the currency of the day.

In spite of the growing resentment and hostility by the older siblings, the younger siblings maintained their unwavering position of independence by establishing their own self-identity, and by holding on to their way of doing things. The younger siblings also refused to emulate or bear any resemblance to their older siblings in any way. In their many acts of defiance, the younger siblings refused to conform to and follow the old established rules of the house as their older siblings. Instead, they established a new set of rules to live by; changed the way they dressed and wore their hair; listened to music and art they preferred; and created their own set of values in every aspect of their lives.

The oldest children were preoccupied with their own self-interests as well while America was busy partying. They had an aura of superiority; they liked war; they liked being in control of trade, finance and economic affairs; and secretly engaged in unfair business practices that gave them the upper hand over everybody else. They gave America false and deceptive permission slips that she unknowingly signed that would later cause the country to have serious problems. They were resistant to America's efforts to implement plans that offered inclusion, ensured fairness, equality, justice, and reconciliation in bringing the family together. The older siblings had their own interests, and were also determined to stick to them. America had a divided household.

Will America decide to transition into the next stage of human growth and development?

America's long term negligence of the social movements that have lasted for over decades bears strong evidence of the social decay that is now surrounding us. There were insidious warning signs of social decaying that surfaced indicating that continual care had been overlooked. Drug dependency is largely responsible for this long term oversight that has covered and hidden serious after birth complications that steadily numbed the pain. The main goal of America was to get relief from her troubling social ills; therefore, emergency attempts were made to address the needs through spending, funding, setting up programs, and hiring numerous caregivers to assist in handling the problems. There were many injuries that went undiagnosed and birth defects that went untreated and undetected. Serious after birth complications had set has grown toxic and requires our immediate and urgent care. We are well aware of the challenges that lie in front of us by our unmet social needs, and we must be willing to roll up our sleeves and do the work of re-claiming our troubled nation. America at this stage can no longer make childish and immature decisions in our needed recovery efforts. Every American must acknowledge that the job that began in the 1960s didn't get finished, and we now must finish it. We can and must avoid another social mishap in America that is result of failing to make good decisions.

Repositioning America

From the mistakes that have been made in the past, the unwanted results of the present, and the insight that we have learned tells us that we must go back to re-examine (think) the foundational pillars of the past. We must also re-examine (rethink) the principles that our lives were previously built upon for comparison today; and consciously (think again) make better informed decisions that will help us to adjust and correct our current challenges. Also, taking a step back gives us an opportunity that can help us to regain our lost sense of purpose for life, and to make and set the right priorities for the future. Our collective efforts will break the repetitious cycle of wrong thinking that has gotten us the unfavorable results that now challenge us. With the younger and the older generations working together, side-by-side, and hand-in-hand we can make the right changes that will be for the common good of all.

The next step that is needed to reposition America and

set her back on the right course is our renewal and practice of the basic fundamental principles of truth and honesty. To help us in transforming our nation we must first transform ourselves. By collectively practicing the correct way to *think, rethink and think again* every time we are faced with a daily decision, large or small, it will help us to interrupt our present normal way of thinking, reshape, and form our new attitudes. With this consistent practice in our daily decisions we will gradually break the cycle of unconsciously reinforcing negative thought patterns brick by brick. We will then progressively become more conscious of practicing the correct and right way to think and make good decisions.

Creating a New Vision for America

America now has an open window of many opportunities for all Americans to participate and seize the present moment that not only will cause a shift that will change the course of this nation, but will change our history as well. Imagine how many of our social problems would disappear if children were properly parented. If parents repositioned themselves back into the lives of their children; and made family life more meaningful, what a difference this would make in helping to restore America? What impact would restored family life have on the incarceration rate? Would America's schools once again become the beneficiaries of positive parental engagement? Would the quality of family life be enhanced if fathers were back in the home? Would the fatherless epidemic cease to exist? Would America's families be successful if all working fathers received wages high enough to meet their financial needs and responsibilities? What impact would the dissolution of drug and human trafficking contribute to healing our social problems?

Finally, how would America benefit from a religious system that transformed itself from the old traditional practices of religion into livable spiritual truths and principles that offered people love and hope; taught and provided relevant insight to guide quality decision making; worked closer with other helping professions in restoring and reconciling families; removed gender roles; encouraged creativity; removed religious labels; and was inclusive of all its citizenry? Every system in our country has gotten off track and we must not blame or enter into judgment of the other.

In conclusion, the real culprit of our social frenzy, and the greatest errors and mistakes of our past is the omission and spiritual neglect of our own divinity and self-worth as human beings. Due to this lack and deficiency, America lost its capacity to courageously meet, deter, and to resist the massive onslaught of the harmful social forces in our midst with truth and resiliency. It was a very presumptuous way of thinking to believe that America could be made better without the ongoing leadership and development of the divine compass that is found within each of us. We must remind ourselves that the exclusion of our spiritual development is the missing step that has brought us to face an unthinkable way of life.

FAMILY LIFESTYLES AT A GLANCE

Traditional Family Lifestyles & Values	Modern Family Lifestyles & Values
Male superiority in the home, society, and workplace	Male dominance obsolete in the home, society, and workplace
Men expected to work and take care of women and children	Women no longer viewed as inferior to men
Men were the breadwinners and achievers	Men and/or Women work outside/inside of the home
Men worked outside the home and women stayed home	Men and/or Women are breadwinners and achievers
Men did not participate in homemaking and child rearing	Men and/or Women have professional jobs and careers
Male role-- teach morals, values and disciplinarian	Men and/or Women are single-parent heads of households
Women inferior to men	Men and/or Women are stay-at-home parents
Women could not vote	
Woman's role—homemaker and child rearing	Men and Women share parenting roles
Women expected to stay married and home until nest emptied	Men and Women share homemaking duties
Women not expected to have careers/higher education	Neither parent home for children at the end of school day
Women had lower career/vocational aspiration. Teachers, nurses and secretaries	Technology major parenting tool—babysitter

Traditional Family Lifestyles & Values	Modern Family Lifestyles & Values
(helping professions)	Childcare provided by daycare workers
Women worked part-time odd jobs to earn extra money	Men not expected to be the sole breadwinner and achiever
Women did not have banking accounts or personal credit	Men not expected to be sole provider for women and children
Women prepared girls for subservient roles at home and in society	Women not expected to be solely homemakers and rear children
Mothers were home when children came home from school	Women not expected to be taken care of by men
Typically women did not have a driver's license	Women not expected to be dominated by men
Typically couples were married	Women not expected to have subservient roles
* * * * * * * *	Women not expected to stay home until the nest is empty
Boys given preferential treatment over girls	Common for couples to live together unmarried
Boys offered a college education (same not offered to girls)	Common for children to have unmarried parents
Boys grew up expecting to have jobs and careers	
Boys expected to make lifelong work commitments	

Traditional Family Lifestyles & Values	Modern Family Lifestyles & Values
Girls expected to solely become mothers and homemakers Girls not expected to succeed	* * * * * * * * * * * Parenting practices non biased/non gender oriented Both Girls and Boys are prepared for lifelong work Both Girls and Boys are expected to be successful Both Girls and Boys are offered a college education Both Girls and Boys offered opportunities to become athletes

CHILDREN IN CRISIS

❖ Fatherless Children

- ❖ Abandoned Children /Run Away Children
- ❖ Unsafe Children
- ❖ Homeless Children
- ❖ Child Murderers
- ❖ Alcoholic Children
- ❖ Child Drug Abuser/Dealer
- ❖ Child High School Drop-out
- ❖ Child Sex Offenders
- ❖ Incarcerated Children
- ❖ Child Parents
- ❖ Gay Children
- ❖ Children Gangs
- ❖ Children Robbers and Thieves
- ❖ Child Prostitutes
- ❖ Children Never Parented
- ❖ Illiterate Children
- ❖ Children Without Leadership
- ❖ Children with AIDS –other major health concerns
- ❖ Hungry Children
- ❖ Violent Children
- ❖ Depressed Children
- ❖ Suicidal Children
- ❖ Child Bullies
- ❖ Obese Children
- ❖ Children in Poverty/Unemployed
- ❖ Foster Care Children
- ❖ Child Graduate High School Without Academic Diploma
- ❖ Children Lack Respect for Authority Figures
- ❖ Child Victim of Human Trafficking

CULTURAL CHALLENGES FACING OURCHILDREN

Peers of divorce
Peers who have been abandoned
Peers with single parents
Peers who are unsupervised
Peers with same sex parents
Peers who watch pornography
Peers who are gang members
Peers who don't respect authority figures
Peers with AIDS/ADD/ADHD
Peers with absent fathers
Peers with incarcerated parents
Peers using/selling drugs & alcohol
Peers who are bullies
Peers sexually active
Peers who are homeless/foster homes
Peers who live with grandparents
Peers who are abused sexually, emotionally, physically
Peers with multiple siblings from same father/multiple women
Peers with unmarried parents
Peers with unmarried parents, with children living together same dwelling
Peers whose mother & daughter pregnant same time
Peers with parents who are drug/alcohol addicts
Peers who do not value education/cut class/tardy/drop-out
Peers from multiple religious backgrounds, ethnicity, races, culture
Peers who are lawbreakers
Peers who carry weapons
Peers who commit violent crimes
Peers involved in sex trade and pornography

FACING THE UNTHINKABLE

Not good enough/unimportant	Broken Families/Homes
Feeling unwanted/needed	Low self-esteem
Teen Suicide	Teen Drug/Alcohol Addiction
Same Sex Parents	Gang Membership
No family/home rules-structure	Bullying
Negative Peer Pressure	Teen Sex Addiction
No Respect for Authority	Unmarried Parents
No Responsibility for	Unlimited/Uncensored
Lack of Adult Supervision	Unlimited/Uncensored Media
Lack of Positive Role Models	School Shooting/Violence
Negative Popularity	Fatherlessness
Living with Non biological	Pornography
No gun control	Homelessness
Peer drug dealers	Terrorism
Unenforced discipline by	Teen Incarceration
Deceased Parents	Abortion
*Never parented (biological	Poverty
Addicted Parents	Massive Killing (public)
Kidnapped by parents/others	Divorced Parents
Sexual/Criminal Assault-Abuse	School Drop-Outs
Fear of an ordinary life	Seldom Church Attendance
Self-Absorbed Culture	Child Sex
Entitlement/Celebrity Culture	Child Abandonment
Trend of Narcissism/Hostility	Unavailable/Absentee Parents
Anger/Shame	Teen Pregnancy
Unemployment	Unlimited/Uncensored Music
Adopted/Foster/Grandparents	Unlimited Entertainment
Multi-generational Households	Child Abuse/Neglect
Test Tube Babies	Lack of Character/Positive

REFERENCES

11 Facts About Human Trafficking. (2015 July 15). Retrieved from https://www.dosomething.org/facts/11-facts-about-human-trafficking

70s Culture: Changes and Events in Seventies Culture. Retrieved from http://www.classic70s.com/70s-culture.html

1990s News, Events, Popular Culture and Prices. Retrieved from http://www.thepeoplehistory.com/1990s.html

(1998). *Rock and Roll Generations: Teen Life in the 50s.* New York: Time Life, Inc.

(2005). *The Sixties: The Years That Shaped a Generation.* New York: PBS Broadcasting.

(2007, April 2007). *1960s Hippies.* Smultz's Channel.

(2013). *Regeneration.* New York: PBS Broadcasting.

(2013, April*). The '80s: The Decade That Made Us.* New York: PBS Broadcasting.

(2013). The *Sixties.* New York: PBS Broadcasting.

(2014, August 14). *Sex, Drugs and Rock N' Roll.* Atlanta: CNN News.

(2014, November). *The '90s: The Last Great Decade.* New York: PBS Broadcasting.

Americas Best History US Timeline, 1980-1989. Retrieved from http://www.americasbesthistory.com/abhtimeline1980.html

Americas Best History US Timeline, 1990-1999. Retrieved from http://www.americasbesthistory.com/abhtimeline1990.html

American Cultural History 1960s. Retrieved from ftp://ftp.heritageacademics.com/ET/.../AMCultHist.pdf

Blankenhorn, D. (1995). *Fatherless America: Confronting Our Most Urgent Social Problem.* New York: Basic Books.

Brokaw, T. (2007). *Boom!: Voices of the Sixties.* New York: Random House.

Brunner, B. (2005*). Time Almanac 2006.* Upper Saddle River:

New Jersey.

Ella, J. *Hippies.* (2007). New York: PBS Broadcasting.

Falsetti, L.A. (2010). Eight Stages of Psychological Development.
Retrieved from
http://docslide.us/documents/erik-erikson-presentation.html

Fullerton, H. N. Labor Force Participation: 75 Years of Change, 1950-
1998 and 1998-2025. Retrieved from
http://www.bls.gov/mlr/1999/12/art1full.pdf

Goodman, W. (1995, August). Boom in the Daycare industry the result
of many social changes. *Monthly Labor Review,* 3-12. Retrieved from
http://www.bls.gov/mlr/1995/08/art1full.pdf.

Grossman, A. Working Mothers With Children. (1981). Special Labor
Force Report Summaries. *Monthly Labor Review*, 50-54. Retrieved
from http://www.bls.gov/opub/mlr/1981/05/rpt3full.pdf
Holmes. (2000). Births to Unwed Mothers. U.S.A. Today.

Bureau of Justice Statistics. (2015*). Juvenile Incarceration.*
Retrieved from http://ojjdp.ncjrs.org/ojstabb/qa135.html

Kahn, A., George-Warren, H., Dahl, S. (Eds.) (1998). *Rolling Stone the
'70s.* New York: Little brown.

Noisbitt, J., Aburdene, P. (1990). *Megatrends 2000: Ten New
Directions for the 1990's.* William Morrow & Co.

Moments in America. (2015, May 25). Retrieved from
http://www.childrensdefense.org/library/moments-in-
america.html

Morris, C. (2014). *Porn Industry Feeling Upbeat About 2014.* Retrieved
from http://www.nbcnews.com/business/business-news/porn-
industry-feeling-upbeat-about-2014-n9076

National Center for Juvenile Justice. *Fact Sheet.* Retrieved from
http://www.nccp.org/publications/pdf/text_1038.pdf

Paulk, E. (1988). *Spiritual Megatrends: Christianity in the 21st
Century.* Charlotte, NC: Kingdom Publishers.

Popenoe, D. (1996). A World Without Fathers. *Wilson Quarterly.*
Retrieved from
189

http://archive.wilsonquarterly.com/essays/world-without-fathers

Schuller, R. (1982). *Self-esteem: The New Reformation*. New York: World Press Books.

Americas Best History US Timeline, 1970-1979. Retrieved from http://www.americasbesthistory.com/abhtimeline_1970.html

Shreve, A. (1987). *Remaking Motherhood: How Working Mothers Are Shaping Our Children's Future*. New York: Viking Penguin.

The 1960s. Retrieved from www.history.com/topics/1960s

The sixties: Pop Culture. Retrieved from http://www.pbs.org/opb/thesixties/topics/culture/

1970s news, events, popular culture and prices. Retrieved from http://www.thepeoplehistory.com/1970s.html.

1980s News, Events, Popular Culture and Prices. Retrieved from http://www.thepeoplehistory.com/1980s.html

The 1980s. Retrieved from www.history.com/topics/1980s

The 1990s. Retrieved from www.history.com/topics/1990s

The Social Issues Research Center (2011). *The Changing Face of Motherhood*. (2011). Proctor & Gamble.

Unmarried Births to Women. (2015, January 15). *National Vital Statistics Reports, 64*(1). Retrieved from http://www.cdc.gov/nchs/data/nvsr/nvsr63/nvsr63_04.pdf

Ventura, S.J., Mathews, T.J., and Hamilton, B.E. Births to Teenagers in the United States, 1940-2000. *National Vital Statistics Reports*, 2-24. Retrieved from http://www.cdc.gov/nchs/data/nvsr/nvsr49/nvsr49_10.pdf

Vital Statistics of the United States & National Vital Statistics Report. Table 78. Retrieve from http://www.census.gov/comperdia/statab/2012/tables/12,0078.pdf

Working Moms. Retrieved from http://www.healthofchildren.com/U-Z/Working-Mothers.html
190

WWW.VL:HISTORY:USA:1970-1979. Retrieved from
http://vlib.iue.it/history/USA/ERAS/20TH/1960s.html

WWW.VL:HISTORY:USA:1960-1969. Retrieved from
http://vlib.iue.it/history/USA/ERAS/20TH/1960s.html

Youth Suicide. Retrieved from
http://www.cdc.gov/violenceprevention/pub/youth_suicide.html

www.ingramcontent.com/pod-product-compliance
Lightning Source LLC
Chambersburg PA
CBHW051041030426
42339CB00006B/139